THIRTEEN HOMILIES OF

Sᴛ AUGUSTINE

ON ST JOHN XIV

THIRTEEN HOMILIES OF

Sᴛ AUGUSTINE

ON ST JOHN XIV.

IN IOH. EV. TRACTATUS LXVII—LXXIX.

WITH TRANSLATION AND NOTES

BY

H. F. STEWART, M.A.

CHAPLAIN OF TRINITY COLLEGE, CAMBRIDGE,
FORMERLY VICE-PRINCIPAL OF THE SALISBURY THEOLOGICAL COLLEGE.

SECOND EDITION

CAMBRIDGE :
AT THE UNIVERSITY PRESS.
1902

CAMBRIDGE
UNIVERSITY PRESS

University Printing House, Cambridge CB2 8BS, United Kingdom

Published in the United States of America by Cambridge University Press, New York

Cambridge University Press is part of the University of Cambridge.

It furthers the University's mission by disseminating knowledge in the pursuit of
education, learning and research at the highest international levels of excellence.

www.cambridge.org
Information on this title: www.cambridge.org/9781107694835

First edition 1900
Second edition 1902
First published 1902
First paperback edition 2014

A catalogue record for this publication is available from the British Library

ISBN 978-1-107-69483-5 Paperback

PREFACE.

THE present edition—the only English one—has been prepared with special regard to the Preliminary Examination of Candidates for Holy Orders, in which these thirteen Homilies form the Latin subject for the years 1901, 1902.

The notes are intended to meet the requirements of the ordinary candidate for that examination, and reference is only made to such books as may reasonably be supposed to be within his reach.

It did not seem necessary to re-tell the familiar story of St Augustine in literary form, but the "Introductory Notes" give concisely the main facts of his life, and his characteristics as a teacher and preacher. An English translation has been added, both for the sake of increasing the practical usefulness of the work, and also because it is in many ways the most convenient and compendious form of commentary on small grammatical points with which it is undesirable to burden the notes. A special section has been devoted to the grammar and language of Augustine and Jerome for the benefit of students who are unfamiliar with the Latin of the time.

The Biblical text employed by St Augustine has also received attention, and it is hoped that the Table, in which Augustinian, Old Latin, and Vulgate readings are displayed in parallel columns, may serve as material for the solution of a difficult problem, or at least awaken interest in it.

The Latin text of the Homilies is that of the Benedictine edition (Paris, 1839).

The Editor's best thanks are due to the Rev. R. St J. Parry, Fellow of Trinity College, for reading and criticizing the "Hints on Grammar," to Mr F. C. Burkitt, of Trinity College for advice in constructing the "Table of Readings," and to the Rev. J. O. F. Murray, Fellow of Emmanuel College, for constant help and correction in every part, and at every stage, of the work

TRINITY COLLEGE, CAMBRIDGE.
June, 1900.

PREFACE TO SECOND EDITION.

A LARGE number of corrections and improvements have been made in both the notes and translation and the spelling and punctuation of the text, for the bulk of which I am indebted to the kindness and learning of the Rev. E. W. Watson, Rector of Sutton, Bedfordshire.

H. F. S.

TRINITY COLLEGE, CAMBRIDGE.
October, 1902.

CONTENTS.

INTRODUCTORY NOTES.

Authorities.

For the general history,

> Kurtz, *Lehrbuch der Kirchengeschichte*, 1892.
> Robertson, *History of the Christian Church*, Vols. I. and II.
> Milman, *Latin Christianity*, Vols. I. and II.
> Villemain, *L'éloquence chrétienne au 4ième siècle.*

For St Augustine,

> Bright, *Lessons from the lives of three great Fathers.*
>   „   *Anti-pelagian Treatises.*

For further reference,

> Cunningham, *St Austin* (Hulsean lectures).
> Cutts, *Life of St Augustine*, S.P.C.K.
> Loofs, art. "*Augustinus*" in Herzog-Hauck's *Realencyclopädie.*
> Poujoulat, *Vie de St Augustin.*
> Reuter, *Augustinische Studien.*

St Augustine himself tells the story of his life up to his baptism in the *Confessions*, which should be read by every one entering upon a study of his works. There is an excellent translation of Books I—IX., with an introduction, by Dr Bigg, in the "Library of Devotion." The saint's later life is recounted by his friend Possidius, bishop of Calama.

§ 1. *Life and Teaching.*

Aurelius Augustinus, born at Thagaste in Numidia (A.D. **354**), of mixed parentage, father a pagan, mother Monnica, a devout Christian [for Christianity and the Church in Africa, see Hort, *Ante-Nicene Fathers*, lect. v.; Lightfoot, *Philippians*, pp. 224, 240, 260; Mullinger, *Ancient African Church*]; educated at University of Carthage, capital of proconsular Africa, second city of the empire, wealthy, cultivated, corrupt. [See Villemain, p. 367; Benson, *Cyprian*, Introd.]

Neither dissipated student life nor worldly ambition—the bar and rhetoric both offered dazzling prizes—could stifle higher intellectual interests, in pursuit of which he read the *Hortensius* of Cicero (a lost treatise in praise of philosophy). This awoke the thirst for truth, which he vainly sought to satisfy by the doctrines of the Manichees (Christianity grafted on Parseeism), although he was associated with them for nine years as catechumen (A.D. **374—383**).

After teaching at Thagaste and Carthage, he seeks a quieter sphere at Rome (A.D. **383**), and thence is appointed public lecturer in rhetoric at Milan (A.D. **384**). Here he studied Neo-platonism, which, while it taught him certain truths about the nature of God, viz., that He is a Spirit, an Unity, yet capable of personal distinctions (the Good, the Intelligence, the Soul), was powerless to touch his conscience. This was effected mainly by the preaching of St Ambrose—not apparently by personal contact with him. For the story of his actual conversion, see *Conf.* viii. 8—12.

(A.D. **387**) Baptism of Augustine and of his natural son, Adeodatus, and death of Monnica who had followed him to Italy. He returns to Rome, where he begins a seven years' controversy with his former allies, the **Manichees.** He meets their chief errors, viz. (1) dualism, (2) essential evil of matter and consequent irresponsibility of man, (3) rejection of the O.T., by maintaining (1) the absolute sovereignty of God, (2) personal responsibility of the individual, (3) continuity of O. and N.T.

Back to Africa and to an ascetic life at Thagaste and the study of philosophy and theology (A.D. **388**).

Ordained priest against his will at Hippo Regius by Bishop Valerius, a Greek, who needed help in preaching Latin (A.D. **391**).

(A.D. **395**) Consecrated bishop coadjutor to Valerius, whose death in A.D. **396** leaves him sole bishop of Hippo.

The period of his episcopate is also that of his chief theological and literary activity.

In active controversy with the **Donatists** (A.D. **400**).

[Donatism (for early history, see Robertson, I., p. 279; in 4th cent. ib. II., p. 127) was a schism peculiar to Africa, where its rigorism found congenial soil. Cp. the success of Montanism there in the time of Tertullian (Hort, *Ante-Nic. Ff.*, lect. v.). The main Donatist contentions, viz., the essential purity of the Church and consequent exclusion of unworthy members (a revival of Novatianism, cp. Robertson, I., p. 170), were met by Augustine (*a*) by conference and argument, in which he shewed

(1) that in the visible Church evil and good are ever mingled (cp. Mt. xiii., parable of the tares and wheat),

(2) that sacraments are not invalidated by the unworthiness of ministers (*ostenditur non ipsos id agere sed per eos utique Spiritum sanctum*),

and (*b*) when argument failed, by persecution (*coge intrare*).]

Great defence of Christianity in the *de Civitate Dei* (A.D. **413**), written against those who attributed to it public calamities, such as the fall of Rome in A.D. **410**.

No sooner were the Donatists crushed by the Conference of Carthage in A.D. **411** and the repressive imperial edicts of A.D. **414, 415**, than the **Pelagian** heresy reared its head, denying

(1) the necessity, though not the advantage, of divine grace (*quod per liberum homines facere iubentur arbitrium possunt implere per gratiam*), and

(2) the transmission of original sin (*Peccatum Adae ipsum solum laesit et non genus humanum...Non propagine sed exemplo.* Cp. *imitatio Adae* "the following of Adam," Article IX.).

Against these doctrines (largely due to the character of Pelagius the recluse, sheltered from the world and its temptations) Augustine, with deeper knowledge both of man and of God (cp. Illingworth, *Personality*, pp. 14, 71 f., 212 f.), maintained (1) the solidarity of the race (*Adam unus est, in quo omnes peccaverunt quando omnes ille unus homo fuerunt*), and (2) the absolute need of prevenient and cooperating grace (*nolentem praevenit ut velit; volentem subsequitur ne frustra velit*).

Augustine's teaching was endorsed by the Synod of Carthage in A.D. **418**, which condemned Pelagianism.

[On Pelagianism, see Bright, *Anti-Pel. Treatises*, Introduction.]

In the course of the Pelagian controversy Augustine developed his final theory of **Predestination**, which may be contrasted with other systems as follows:

b 2

(*a*) God has predestinated some of mankind to life)(ecclesiastical privileges (Clem. Rom., Ignatius).

(*b*) This predestination is arbitrary, according to His inscrutable will)(doctrine of prevision, *ex praevisis meritis* (Clem. Alex., Origen, Chrysostom and Arminianism).

(*c*) Only the predestinated can be saved)(Universalists.

(*d*) None can tell with absolute certainty whether he is saved)(Calvinism, Lambeth Arts. 6.

At the bottom of Augustine's theory lies the idea of the Divine omnipotence. He tried to reconcile the existence of evil with this by the supposition that good and evil together enhanced God's glory more than good alone, because evil displayed His power in punishment.

> [For development of Augustinian theory into double predestination, to life and to damnation, by Gottschalc and Calvin, see Gibson, *On the Articles*, p. 475 ff., and on the whole question, Mozley, *Augustinian Theory of Predestination.*]

Invasion of Africa by Arian Vandals (A.D. **428**).

(A.D. **430**) Death of Augustine (aet. 76) during the siege of Hippo.

§ 2. *The Homilies on St John.*

These homilies on St John's Gospel were

(1) probably delivered in the year A.D. **416** (Augustine's best period),

(2) as a course of sermons covering the greater part of the year,

(3) beginning in Lent.

In proof of these three points we may note

(1) the frequent references to Pelagianism, which was rife between the years A.D. **411** and **418** (see above, § 1), and the allusion to the finding of the supposed relics of St Stephen, which may be placed in A.D. **415** (*Tr.* cxx. 4). Cp. *Dict. Christ. Antiq.* III. p. 1929.

(2) Augustine more than once speaks of them as a connected course [*ab ipso principio usque ad hodiernam lectionem quae supra dicta sunt meministis iam esse tractata* (*Tr.* xiii. 1); *Evangelium secundum Ioannem ex ordine lectionum nos solemus tractare* (*Prol. Tr. in Ep. Ioan.*)], the wide range of which appears from the fact that, while *Tr.* vi. 1 mentions winter cold [*fateor, timueram ne*

frigus hoc vos frigidos ad conveniendum faceret], the preacher had not got beyond *Tr.* xxvii. on August 10, the festival of St Laurence [*cuius hodie festa celebramus (Tr.* xxvii. 12)].

(3) *Tr.* x. 1 states that Easter is near [*ipsius templi solutionem et reaedificationem anniversaria solemnitate celebraturi sumus*], and in *Prol. Tr. in Ep. Ioan.* Augustine alludes to the interruption of his course on the Gospel of St John by the occurrence of Easter (see below, p. xiv), and in *Tr.* xiii. 1 to its resumption after the festival.

The homilies afford a valuable illustration of (*a*) the character of the sermon in the early Church, and (*b*) of St Augustine's mingled power and weakness as a preacher.

(*a*) **The Sermon in the Early Church.**

The main object of public worship in apostolic times was edification (see 1 Cor. xiv., esp. *v.* 17). This was then secured by prophecy, which was didactic rather than predictive (see Lightfoot, *Notes on Epistles*, p. 83).

On the withdrawal of the Pentecostal gifts, the element of edification was chiefly supplied by the sermon or exposition (see Justin M., I. *Apol.* 67). Hence its prominence in the service of the Church everywhere except at Rome (see Duchesne, *Origines du culte chrétien*, p. 163).

The exercise of miraculous gifts carrying their own Divine sanction was apparently permitted to any member of the congregation; but when the Church systematized her service and felt the need of emphasizing her essential unity, she vested the right of preaching (as also of celebrating the Eucharist) in the bishop, by whom however it was often extended to a presbyter, acting as his representative, occasionally to a deacon, and in rare instances to a layman (cp. the case of Origen at Caesarea, Robertson, I., p. 143).

Augustine, who owed his ordination as presbyter largely to his capacity to preach in Latin (see above, § 1), was after his consecration fully sensible of his episcopal prerogative (see *Sermo* cccxxix.[1] preached on the anniversary of his consecration).

The sermon's place in the service was in the *Missa Catechumenorum* (= ante-communion service) after the *lectiones*. Of these

---

[1] References to Augustine are to the Paris (1839) reprint of the Benedictine edition.

there were at least two (Epistle or Prophet, and Gospel), sometimes three (Epistle, Prophet, and Gospel) or four (Epistle, Prophet,
Acts, and Gospel). The early practice was to read whole books of
the Bible in course (*lectio continua*) at the discretion of the bishop,
but the development of the ecclesiastical year of feasts and obser-
vances brought in the proper lection (*lectio propria*), especially in
the Western Church. Thus while, apart from other evidence, these
Homilies clearly shew that the bishop could generally control the
lectionary (cp. *Tr.* xlvi. 1 where Sunday's Gospel is ordered to be
repeated on a week day), they also prove abundantly that the
Gospel for certain days was already fixed by custom (cp. *Tr.* xi. 1,
where the congregation is congratulated on the coincidence of the
Gospel for the day with the theme of the preacher), and Augustine
in the prologue to his homilies on the First Epistle of St John states
that his course upon the Gospel, following, though evidently not
pari passu, a prescribed order of lections, was interrupted by the
occurrence of Holy Week, when the Church always read the story
of the Passion in the words of the different Evangelists. (See
above, p. xiii.) The facts seem to be that St John's Gospel was read
in the North African Church during Lent, and that Augustine
availed himself of the opportunity of beginning a course of sermons
upon it, not necessarily confining himself to the Gospel for the day,
and sometimes exercising his right as bishop to order the lection.

Sermons thus based upon and following immediately after a con-
tinuous passage of Scripture would naturally be more in the nature
of connected exposition and application than set discourse. Their
informal character is illustrated by the ordinary Greek name ὁμιλία
(ὁμιλεῖν = to converse with, cp. ὡμίλουν πρὸς ἀλλήλους, Lk. xxiv.
11), of which *tractatus* is the recognized Latin equivalent (see
Tr. lxvii., note 1). The freedom and familiarity of the sermon was
reflected in the behaviour of the audience, which everywhere, except
perhaps at Rome, was quite open in its expressions of approval,
emotion, or attentiveness. That this last was not always exem-
plary is indicated by Augustine's frequent exclamations, *erigenda
anima* (e.g. *Tr.* lxvii. 1), *erectis auribus audite, intendite, attendite,
adestote toto animo*, etc., and by the words with which the deacon
introduced the Gospel, in the east πρόσχωμεν, in the west *state
cum silentio, audientes intente* (see Duchesne, *Origines*, p. 162); but
discipline in N. Africa and at Rome was generally too good to call

forth such reproofs as we meet with in the pages of Origen and Chrysostom.

The lection was delivered from the *ambo* or reading-pew by the reader (*lector*) or deacon ; the people sat, except for the Gospel, when they rose and remained standing (except in Italy) during the sermon, which was practically the expansion of the Gospel.   The preacher sat, either in the episcopal chair behind the altar, or at the chancel rails (*cancelli*), or in the *ambo* (see *Dictionary of Christ. Antiq.* I., pp. 72 and 263).   Sermons were, as a rule, not written, and in the case of an ancient rhetor, like Augustine, often not prepared, but extemporized.   (In one of his sermons he declares that he did not determine to preach until the service was already in progress ; the subject is sometimes abruptly changed in the middle of a discourse, and sometimes chosen by means of a *sors biblica.*)   Their preservation is due to the skill of shorthand writers, either amateur or professional (*notarii*, ὀξυγράφοι or ταχυγράφοι).

(*b*)   **Augustine as preacher.**

A fair estimate of Augustine as a preacher may be formed by comparing the ideal he himself has proposed in the *de Doctrina Christiana, lib.* iv. (an ideal which, *mutatis mutandis*, is always true) with its realization in practice.   Illustration of this from these homilies is given below in square brackets.

(*a*)   The preacher's chief business is *tractatio scripturarum*, i.e. the exposition of the truths which he has discovered in the Bible (*de Doctr. Christ.* § 1).

> [The homilies by their form and matter alike support this state-
> ment on every page.]

The sovereign means to sound exposition are the help of the Holy Spirit and prayer (1) for the preacher himself, (2) for his hearers (*orator sit antequam dictor*, § 32).

> [For this, cp. *Tr.* lxix. 2 *quo donante dico...*
>   *ib.* 3 *dic mihi, Dominus meus...*
>   *Tr.* lxxi. 1 *loquentibus nobis sed ipso docente...*
>   *Tr.* lxxiv. 1 *verumtamen quantum...*
>   *Tr.* lxxvi. 3 *intelligamus quantum aperire...*]

(*b*)   In his exposition the preacher must keep in view (1) doctrinal, and (2) moral instruction; enemies must be won to the Faith, weak or doubting brethren must be confirmed and taught (§ 6).

> [The homilies are full of doctrine, but the treatment of the following subjects is specially to be noted:
>> Person and Natures of Christ, *Tr.* lxix. 3; lxxviii.
>> Divinity of Christ, *Tr.* lxxi.
>> Trinity, *Tr.* lxxvii.
>> Holy Spirit, *Tr.* lxxiv.; lxxvi. 4.
>> Predestination, *Tr.* lxviii. 1.
>
> For the conversion of gainsayers, see *Tr.* lxvii. 3 (Pelagians); *Tr.* lxviii. 2 (Donatists); *Tr.* lxx. 2; *Tr.* lxxi. 2 f.; *Tr.* lxxviii. 2 (Sabellians and Arians).
>
> The confirmation and instruction of believers is evidently his consistent aim.]

The preacher must ever vary his method to suit the needs of his audience, employing simple narrative in order to teach, strict logic to prove, and every hortatory device at his command to arouse (§ 6).

The observance of two general maxims is necessary to form a perfect preacher (*a*) *sapienter agere* (indispensable), and (*b*) *eloquenter dicere* (desirable).   The former springs from knowledge of Scripture, not only of the letter, though that will help the want of eloquence, but of the spirit.   Scripture is the source from which the preacher can draw the ornament and grace as well as the substance of his discourse.   The inspired writers indeed must be his model in everything except their obscurity, for clearness and logical sequence (*ut intelligatur*) are his first and last essentials.   He has a criterion of clearness in his hearers; he must never leave a theme or a point until he reads intelligence of it in their demeanour, and to awaken this intelligence he must vary the expression of his thoughts in a way that is hardly possible to one who writes his sermons or learns them by heart.   As soon as ever he feels that he is understood he must change his subject or close his sermon (§ 25).

> [The subject-matter of the Homilies is sufficiently scriptural, and needs no comment.   Of studied imitation of inspired writers there is no trace.   Augustine had no need to borrow eloquence; but many passages have a Pauline fervour (e.g. *Tr.* lxvii. 3; *Tr.* lxxiii. 4; *Tr.* lxxvii. 4), even if some present a Pauline difficulty (e.g. *Tr.* lxxviii. 1).

Obscurity indeed is far from his intention (cp. *Tr.* lxxvii. 4 *erit ipsa brevitas altera obscuritas*). His determination to be understood is evident throughout—*Tr.* lxxvii. opens with a call to attention—and his desire not to fatigue the congregation evinces itself at the close of almost every homily. His patience and logical persistence (*Tr.* lxix. 2; *Tr.* lxxii. 1, 2; *Tr.* lxxviii. 3); his variety and skilful use of analogy (*Tr.* lxix. 4; *Tr.* lxxiii. 3; *Tr.* lxxiv. 5) all have a present value.

But Augustine's great power lies in his fervour. His sermons are great by the character by which George Herbert reckoned greatness in a preacher, viz., holiness, and they attain it by the very means commended by our English saint in his *Country Parson*:

(1) Cordiàl sincerity (evident throughout);

(2) Apostrophes to God (*Tr.* lxvii. 4; *Tr.* lxviii. 3; *Tr.* lxix. 3);

(3) Love of his people (*Tr.* lxvii. 2; *Tr.* lxix. 4; *Tr.* lxxvii. 4);

(4) Direct appeals to them (*Tr.* lxvii. 1; *Tr.* lxix. 2; *Tr.* lxxiii. 3).

His defects are obvious and occur in those very particulars upon which he himself laid stress, (1) method and (2) Bible knowledge. The want of method shewn in the constant repetitions, and the failure to exhaust any single topic, are the inevitable results of improvisation and of a sermon course of indefinite duration. The weakness of exposition is due partly to the circumstances and partly to the nature of the man. For all his learning Augustine was not a great scholar; if he overcame his youthful horror of Greek (see *Conf.* i. 13, 14), Hebrew remained practically sealed to him. And he had not the critical sense. Hence his obvious and inevitable errors of exegesis (e.g. *Tr.* lxviii. 1 on Is. xlv. 11; *Tr.* lxx. 1 on Ps. lxi. 7; *Tr.* lxxvii. 3 *pacem super pacem*; see notes), and his abuse of allegorism. There does not happen to be much of this last in the homilies before us (but cp. *Tr.* lxxvi. 5), though it is rife in the rest of the series; it will therefore be enough to refer to Bigg's *Christian Platonists* (Bampton Lectures), pp. 132—151, and to remark that allegorism is after all the only possible answer of an uncritical age to the difficulties of Scripture; that while there is much in the allegorism of the Fathers that strikes us as puerile, the principle upon which they went was right—every word of

Scripture has a tongue and a meaning—and the conclusions, whether doctrinal or moral, which they reached, are generally sound, although the arguments adduced are often faulty. We admit with Calvin that the true meaning of Scripture is the natural and obvious meaning, that when we are disposed to smile at allegorism we must remember not only St Paul's sanction of it (1 Cor. x. 11; Gal. iv. 24), but also the wealth of parable, metaphor and figure throughout Scripture, and shew respect to a method that exhibits in a marked degree the inscrutable power of the Word of God.]

§ 3. *Augustine's style and language.*

After allegorism the modern critic will be tempted to fasten first on Augustine's faults of taste—the incessant assonance and alliteration, the forced antitheses, the terrible puns—and then on the quality of his Latin.

(*a*) As to the former, the maxim *le style c'est l'homme même* must not be applied too stringently or universally; that would include Augustine and all his contemporaries in one condemnation. Remember that the taste of a writer is generally that of his age, that the affectations that shock us were the delight of the 5th century, and notice how often Augustine rises superior to them all, never allowing an appeal to the head to supplant one to the heart.

(*b*) His Latin must not be contemptuously dismissed as "ecclesiastical"; it is the living language of his time and is of equal interest (1) to the philological, and (2) to the theological student.

(1) It certainly lacks the breadth and grandeur of the ancient, and the symmetry and clearness of modern, languages, but it is not altogether without the advantages that belong to both. Thus, while it preserves almost intact the freedom and suppleness which the former owe to their inflexions, the analytical qualities of the latter, e.g. French, are already present in germ.

(2) The theological student may draw an interesting parallel between the Latin of the decadence and Hellenistic Greek. Each is separated from the respective classical period by an almost equal space of time; each is admirably suited to the purpose of the Church, viz., the proclamation and exposition of the Gospel. It is not too much to say that neither St Paul nor St Augustine could have secured so wide and so immediate a hearing if they had written like Plato and Cicero.

Augustine's sermons however do not owe their influence and vitality only to the suitable character or the vehicle which conveyed them, nor even to the depth and greatness of their thought. They deserve to live merely as literature. They contain many passages of matchless tenderness and majesty, and they set the style for theological writing which was followed throughout the middle ages.

§ 4. *Augustine's Bible text.*

The Latin Bible with which we are familiar, St Jerome's Vulgate, was of course not the first in the field. Certainly in the 3rd century probably by the middle of the 2nd century, possibly in Jewish circles even before Christian times, there were translations of the Scriptures into African Latin. Translations, not translation, for though we are accustomed to speak of the Old Latin Version there was no single authoritative version. It was indeed the variety and confusion caused by many independent translators and the carelessness of copyists that induced Damasus, bishop of Rome (A.D. 366—384), to commission Jerome to retranslate the Bible into Latin. Jerome set to work at once, and issued the Gospels in A.D. 384, and the rest of both O. and N.T. before A.D. 405. Thus at the time when Augustine was preaching these homilies (416, see above, p. xii), the whole of the Bible in the new version must have been in his hands.

What was his attitude towards it? It seems to have been hesitating. He welcomed the revision of the Gospels and congratulated Jerome upon it (*proinde non parvas Deo gratias agimus de opere tuo quod Evangelium ex Graeco interpretatus es, quia paene in omnibus nulla offensio est. Ep.* civ. *ad Hier.* A.D. 403), but he did not extend this approval to his treatment of the O.T. Holding, in common with his contemporaries, the LXX. to be as really inspired as the Hebrew original, he deprecated any fresh translation which would seem to lower the authority of the Greek, and he refused to allow Jerome's version to be publicly read in Church *ne...magno scandalo perturbemus plebes Christi* (*Ep.* cxvi. 35)[1].

---

[1] That the danger was a real one is shewn by the story of the tumult raised by a certain African congregation against their bishop when a new word for Jonah's gourd (*hedera* instead of *cucurbita*) fell upon their ears. Cp. Aug. *Epp.* lxxi.; lxxxii.

Evidence is indeed not wanting that Augustine finally came to value the new translation as a whole, but to the end of his life he continued to use the Old Latin for the O.T. ; and while in writing he frequently had recourse to the Vulgate, his pulpit quotations do not correspond to any particular form of extant text, but follow sometimes the Vulgate, sometimes the O.L., and sometimes the inexact suggestions of the preacher's memory[1].

Some idea of his Bible text may be formed by consulting the subjoined table, in which, parallel to Augustine's quotations in these 13 homilies, are set the Vulgate variants, and such Old Latin readings as can be recovered from African writers and texts. The chief African authorities available for our purpose are—

1. Pseudo-Augustine, *Speculum* (quoted as *m*).
2. Cyprian (A.D. **200—258**).
3. Optatus, bishop of Mileva (c. **368**).
4. Tyconius the Donatist († **390**). See Burkitt, *The Rules of Tyconius* (Cambr. Texts and Studies, III. 1).
5. Faustus and Felix the Manichees, whose Biblical quotations are preserved in Augustine's writings against them.

N.B. Tertullian († **230**) is excluded from the list by the uncertainty as to whether he translated straight from the Greek or used an existing Latin version.

The African texts used for the purpose of our comparison are—

k codex Bobbiensis, containing portions of Mark and Matthew (edited by H. J. White in Part II. of *Old Latin Biblical Texts*).

e codex Palatinus (portions of Matthew and Mark and almost the whole of John and Luke).

h the Fleury palimpsest (portions of Acts and Catholic Epistles), edited by Berger, *Le palimpseste de Fleury*. Paris, 1889.

---

[1] His quotations from the book (e.g. in announcing the text of a sermon) appear to be taken from the Vg.; those from memory often correspond more closely to the O.L. The whole subject is a very interesting one and reference should be made to Burkitt, *The Old Latin and the Itala* (Cambridge Texts and Studies, IV. 3); the *Epilogus* to the *Oxford Vulgate*, p. 656, and Burkitt's review of the same (*Journal of Theological Studies*, Vol. I. p. 129 ff.); Westcott's article on the Vulg. in Smith's *Dictionary of the Bible*, III. p. 1688 ff.

AUGUSTINE'S BIBLICAL QUOTATIONS IN *TRACTATUS IN JOAN.* LXVII—LXXIX. COMPARED WITH AFRICAN AND VULGATE READINGS.

The African column is left blank only when there is no African reading to record. The Vulgate column is left blank when the reading corresponds with Augustine.

An isolated symbol or name in the African column (and for the Psalms in African and Vulgate columns) indicates correspondence with Augustine.

A few readings other than African which seem to deserve notice are indicated by the symbol of the MSS which contain them, and placed in the African column within brackets.

½ after a name means once out of two occurrences. See Westcott and Hort, *Notes on Select Readings*, p. 6.

N.B.   *k* = codex Bobbiensis.
       e = codex Palatinus.
       h = Fleury palimpsest.
       m = *Speculum.*

See p. xx.

AFRICAN LATIN	AUGUSTINE	VULGATE
	2 KINGS	
	ii. 9. *Spiritus qui est in te duplo*	ut fiat in me duplex spiritus tuus
	sit in me	

AFRICAN LATIN	AUGUSTINE PSALMS[1]	VULGATE
Cypr.	ii. 7. Dominus dixit ad me, Filius meus es tu	*GRH*
	ix. 35. *Pupillo* tu *eris* adiutor	R, orphano *G* ; factus es *H*
	xvii. 2. Diligam te, Domine, *virtus mea*	R, fortitudo *GH*
	xli. 7. *Ad me ipsum turbata est anima mea*	anima mea conturbata est *G*, a me ipso anima mea turbata est *R*, in memetipso anima mea incurvatur *H*
	xlii. 1. Iudica me, Deus, et discerne causam meam *de* gente non sancta	*RG* a *H*
	lxvii. 7. *facit unanimes habitare* in domo	R (h. f. u.) inhabitare facit unius moris *G* solitarios *H*
inhabitare facit unanimes *Cypr.*	lxviii. 5. quae non *rapui* tunc *exsolvebam*	*RG*, rapueram...reddebam *H*

[1] The Vg column contains the reading of the Psalter, R = *Psalterium romanum*, his first revision of the O.L., issued about 383 A.D., G = *Psalterium gallicanum*, his second revision 387 A.D., which is the form in which the Psalms appear in the Vulgate, and H = *Psalterium juxta hebraicam veritatem*, 392—3 A.D., which never came into general use. See Kirkpatrick, *Psalms*, Bk I (*Cambridge Bible for Schools*), Intr. p. lv. Westcott, art. "Vulgate" in Smith's *Dictionary of the Bible*, and White, art. "Vulgate" in Hastings's *Dictionary of the Bible*.

de Cypr.	lxxxiii. 5. Beati qui habitant in domo tua : *in saecula saeculorum laudabunt te*	G
		tua+domine: in saeculum saeculi R
		adhuc H
mihi tribuit *Cypr.*	cxv. 12. Quid *retribuam domino pro omnibus quae retribuit mihi*	GR, reddam...tribuit H
	cxxii. 1. Ad te levavi *animam meam qui habitas in caelo*	oculos meos GRH
		caelis H

ISAIAH

et si non credideritis neque intelligitis *Cypr.*	vii. 9[1]. *Nisi enim credideritis non intelligetis*	si non credideritis non permanebitis
	xlv. 11. *Qui fecit quae futura sunt* (LXX. ὁ ποιήσας τὰ ἐπερχόμενα)	(haec dicit Dominus sanctus Israel) plastes eius : ventura interrogate me
	lviii. 9. *pacem super pacem*	pacem, pacem

WISDOM

	ix. 15. *corpus quod corrumpitur aggravat animam et deprimit terrena inhabitatio* sensum multa cogitantem	corpus+enim
		depr. terr. inh.

[1] In *de Doctr. Christ.* ii. 17 Aug. shews how the two readings *intelligetis* and *permanebitis* illustrate each other. See note on *Tr.* lxix. § 1, and Burkitt, *The Old Latin and the Itala*, p. 61.

AFRICAN LATIN	AUGUSTINE	VULGATE
	St Matthew	
Felices mundi *Cypr.* puro *Faustus*	v. 8. *Beati mundo corde quia ipsi Deum videbunt*	
	vi. 9. Pater noster qui *es* in caelis	
Opt. Cypr. om es *k* / veniat *k*	vi. 10. *veniat* regnum tuum	adveniat
Opt. remitte *k Cypr.* ½	vi. 12. *dimitte* nobis debita nostra	
passus fueris induci nos *k* patiaris nos induci *Cypr.*	vi. 13. ne *nos inferas* in tentationem	inducas nos
om haec *Cypr.* sermones meos…eos *m* fecit *k* illum *k* similem aestimabo eum *m* sapienti *k Cypr.* aedificavit *k m Cypr.* super *k m Cypr.* ½	vii. 24. *Qui audit verba mea haec et facit ea similabo eum viro prudenti qui aedificat domum suam supra petram*	assimilabitur / sapienti ; aedificavit
venient autem dies quando auferetur *k*	ix. 15. *veniet hora ut auferatur ab eis sponsus et tunc ieiunabunt filii sponsi*	venient autem dies cum auferetur
om filii sponsi *k* / similatum est *k*	xiii. 24. *simile est* regnum caelorum homini *seminanti* bonum semen in agro suo	*om* filii sponsi / simile factum est / qui seminavit
e vero *m* semen inquit *k*	xiii. 38. bonum *autem semen hi sunt filii regni*	vero
filius hominis *m e k* / colligunt *e k* congregabunt *m*	xiii. 41. mittet *in fine rex ipse* angelos suos et *colligent* de regno eius omnia scandala	filius hominis

magister vester unus est Christus

om enim
transibunt

possidete
Sp. + quidem

erat subditis illis

---

xiii. 43. Tunc iusti fulgebunt sicut sol in regno patris sui

xxiii. 10. *Unus est magister vester Christus*

xxiv. 35. caelum *enim* et terra *transibit*

xxv. 34. Venite, benedicti patris mei, *percipite regnum*

xxvi. 41. *Spiritus* promptus est, caro autem infirma

St Luke

ii. 40. Puer autem crescebat et con- *fortabatur plenus sapientia*, et *gratia Dei erat in illo*

ii. 51. *illis subditus erat*

iv. 18. Spiritus Domini super me propter quod unxit me, *evangelizare* pauperibus misit me

St John

i. 1. In principio *erat verbum*, et *verbum* erat apud Deum, et Deus erat *verbum*

---

k
mei e
S. A. quoniam mag. est vobis Chr. e

om enim e
transiet e
regnum + quod vobis paratum est Opt. Cypr.

corroborabatur adcrescebat et im- plebat sapientia e
super illum e
fuit subjectus illis e

bene nuntiare e

c m e fuit sermo Cypr. 3

AFRICAN LATIN	AUGUSTINE	VULGATE
	ST JOHN	
ipsum e Cypr.	i. 10. et mundus per *eum* factus est	ipsum
Tyc. facta e (b)	i. 14. verbum caro *factum* est	
nec e	iii. 34. *non* enim ad mensuram dat Deus spiritum	
om Deus e (b f l)		
quae enim pater facit eadem et filius facit e	v. 19. *quaecunque pater facit haec et filius similiter* facit	quaecunque enim ille fecerit
quomodo enim e sicut enim m ita e	v. 21. *sicut* pater suscitat mortuos et vivificat, *sic* et filius quos vult vivificat	sicut + enim
quomodo e pater habet vitam in se e Tyc.	v. 26. *Sicut enim habet pater vitam in semetipso,* sic dedit filio *habere vitam in semetipso*	pater habet
vitam habere in se Tyc.		vitam habere
audit e	vi. 45. Omnis qui *audivit* a patre et didicit venit ad me	
Tyc. Cypr. Ego + enim m et ego et pater meus e	x. 30. *Ego et pater* unum sumus	
Cypr. etsi e	xi. 25. Qui credit in me *licet moriatur* vivet (vide *Tr.* lxxii. 2 not.)	etiamsi mortuus fuerit
priusquam gallus cantet e negabis e	xiii. 38. *Non cantabit gallus* donec *ter me neges*	me ter
conturbetur c. v. neque trepidet e Deo e	xiv. 1. Non *turbetur* cor vestrum, *credite in Deum,* et in me credite	creditis (credite D = Book of Armagh E = Codex Egertonensis)

xiv. 2. In domo patris mei *mansiones multae sunt*, si quo minus,
dixissem vobis *quia vado parare*
vobis locum

xiv. 3. Et si abiero et *praeparavero
vobis locum*, iterum *venio* et *accipiam vos* ad me ipsum, ut *ubi*
sum ego et vos sitis

xiv. 4. Et *quo ego vado* (quo vado)
scitis et viam *scitis*

xiv. 5. *Dicit ei* Thomas : Domine
nescimus quo *vadis* et quomodo
possumus viam scire?

xiv. 6. *Dicit ei* Jesus : Ego sum *via*
et veritas et vita : nemo venit
ad patrem nisi per me

xiv. 7. Si *cognovistis* me, et patrem
meum *utique cognovistis* (om.
utique ⅔), et amodo *cognoscetis*
eum et *vidistis* eum

xiv. 8. *Dicit ei* Philippus : Domine,
ostende nobis patrem et sufficit
nobis

xiv. 9. *Dicit ei* Jesus : tanto tempore *vobiscum sum* et non *cognovistis* me, Philippe? *Qui videt*

Apparatus (left column):

multae sunt mansiones *e*

eo *e*

paravero iterum veniam et sumam
vos ut sicubi etc. *e*

et scitis quo eam et viam nostis *e*

Dixit *m* ait Th. *e*
non scimus *m e* eas *m e*
viam novimus Tert. *m e* (*a*) scimus (*b*)
Cypr. e ait illi *m e* ego sum ianua et
via et ver. *Opt.*

om utique *m e* (*a b c d lf f*)
cognoscitis *e* nostis *m*
illum *e* videtis *m e*
ait Ph. *e* ait illi *m*

dixit *m* ait illi Jesus *e*

nostis *e*

c 2

Margin (right column, at xiv. 7):

cognovissetis
cognovissetis
cognoscitis

AFRICAN LATIN	AUGUSTINE	VULGATE
	St John	
me vidit vidit *m* vidit patrem *e*	me (me videt ½) *videt* et pa-trem. Quomodo tu dicis, os-tende nobis patrem?	vidit me vidit
creditis *m* quoniam *e*	xiv. 10. Non *credis quia* ego in patre, et pater in me est? Verba quae ego *loquor vobis a me ipso non loquor, pater autem in me manens ipse facit opera*	
dico *e om* ipso *e* non a me loquor *m* sed pater *m* loquitur et opera quae facio ipse facit *m* facit facta *e*		
credite mihi *e m* si quo minus *e m* + vel *m* ipsa opera *m* facta ipsa *e*	xiv. 11. *Non creditis quia* ego in patre et pater in me est? *Alioquin propter opera ipsa* credite	
in me credit facta *e* *om* et mai. hor. faciet *e* quia vado ad patrem meum *e*	xiv. 12. Amen amen dico vobis, qui *credit in me, opera quae ego facio et ipse faciet, et maiora horum faciet, quia ego ad patrem vado*	
quidquid *e*	xiv. 13. Et *quaecunque* (quodcunque) petieritis in nomine meo *haec* (hoc) faciam ut *glorificetur* pater in filio	quodcunque
hoc *e magnificetur e*		hoc
ego *e*	xiv. 14. Si quid *petieritis* in nomine meo *hoc* faciam	petieritis + me

xiv. 15. Si *diligitis* me *mandata* mea servate

xiv. 16. et ego rogabo patrem et alium *paracletum* dabit vobis *ut maneat* vobiscum in aeternum

xiv. 17. spiritum veritatis quem *mundus non potest accipere*, *quia* non videt eum *nec scit* (cognoscit ½) eum; vos autem cognoscetis eum, quia apud vos manebit et in vobis erit

xiv. 18. Non relinquam vos orphanos, *veniam* ad vos

xiv. 19. Adhuc modicum et *mundus me iam non videt*; vos autem videbitis me; *quia ego vivo et vos vivetis*

xiv. 20. In *illo* die *vos cognoscetis quia ego sum* in patre meo et vos in me et ego in vobis

xiv. 21. Qui habet mandata mea et servat (*custodit*) ea, ille est qui *diligit me. Et qui diligit me* diligetur a patre meo, et ego diligam eum et *manifestabo ei me ipsum*

scit

cognoscitis

videtis

servat
qui autem

diligites *e* praecepta *m*

advocatum *e m*
sit *e* qui vobiscum sit *m*

accipere saeculum non potest *e*
quoniam *e* illum *e* non novit illum *e*
nostis *e*
illum *e*
manet *e* est in aeternum *e*

venio *e*
pusillum *e* saeculum me non videbit *e*
om quia...vivetis *e*

illa *e* scietis vos *e*
quoniam sum *e*

illa *e*
me diligit *e* om et qui...me *e*

illum *e* ostendam me ipsum illi *e*

AFRICAN LATIN	AUGUSTINE	VULGATE
	ST JOHN	
om ei e est factum quoniam e incipis manifestare e saeculo e dicit Jesus e me dil. e m verbum e	xiv. 22. Dicit ei Iudas, non ille Iscariotes : Domine quid factum est quia nobis manifestaturus es te ipsum et non mundo? xiv. 23. Respondit Iesus et dixit ei: si quis diligit me, sermonem meum servabit, et pater meus	
diligebit illum et apud illum veniam e faciam e	diliget eum, et ad eum veniemus et mansionem apud eum faciemus	
facit verbum meum non est meum e	xiv. 24. Qui non diligit me, sermones meos non servat et sermo quem audistis non est meus, sed eius qui misit me patris	sermonem
me misit e		
e m	xiv. 25. Haec locutus sum vobis apud vos manens	
advocatus m spiritus autem para-cletus sanctus e pater mittit e docet e admonebit e quae e om vobis e m om omnia...vobis m	xiv. 26. Paracletus autem spiritus sanctus quem mittet pater in nomine meo, ille vos docebit omnia et commemorabit vos omnia quaecunque dixero vobis (vide Tr. lxxvii. 2 not.)	suggeret vobis

relinquo vobis

om ego

xiv. 27. *Pacem vobis relinquo, pacem meam do vobis; non quomodo mundus dat, ego do vobis.* Non turbetur cor vestrum neque *formidet*

xiv. 28. Audistis *quia* ego dixi vobis: vado et venio ad vos: *si diligeretis me* gauderetis *utique quia ego vado ad patrem, quia* pater maior me est

xiv. 29. Et nunc dixi vobis priusquam fiat, ut cum factum fuerit credatis

xiv. 30. Iam non *multa loquar* vobiscum; venit enim princeps *mundi* huius et *in me non habet* quidquam

xiv. 31. Sed ut *cognoscat mundus quia* diligo patrem et *sicut mandatum dedit mihi pater,* sic facio. Surgite eamus hinc

xv. 4. Manete in me et ego in vobis

pacem + meam remitto vobis *e* dimitto *Cypr.* ½ remitto *Cypr.* ½ p. m. do vobis p. m. relinquo vobis *Opt.*
om non...vobis *e*
conturbetur *e*
trepidet *e*
quoniam *e*

si me dilexissetis *Cypr. e*
om utique *Cypr. e*
quoniam ad patrem vado (v. ad p. *Cypr.*) *Cypr. e*
e

loquar multa *e*

saeculi *e* non habet in me *e*

sciat saeculum *e*
quoniam ego *e*
quo modo mand. mihi dedit (*om pater*) *e*

e

AFRICAN LATIN	AUGUSTINE	VULGATE
	St John	
sarmenta *e*	xv. 5. ego sum vitis; *vos palmites*	
e	xv. 5. sine me nihil potestis facere	
e	xvi. 10. ad patrem vado	
inspiravit et ait illis *Cypr.* ⅔ insufflavit...dicens *Cypr.* ⅓	xx. 22. *Insufflans* ait: accipite spiritum sanctum	insufflavit et dicit eis
credis *e* felices *Cypr.*	xx. 29. Quia *vidisti credidisti*; *beati* qui non *vident et credunt* (vide *Tr.* lxxix. 1 not.)	vidisti + me
viderunt et crediderunt *m Cypr. Faust.* credent *e*		viderunt et crediderunt
	Acts	
	i. 11. Sic veniet quemadmodum vidistis eum euntem in caelum	
eis *m*	x. 20. vade cum *illis* (nihil dubitans) quia ego misi *eos*	eis
		illos
	xv. 9. Fide *mundans* corda eorum	purificans
	Romans	
est enim D. *Cypr.* omnis homo mendax solus Deus verax *Felix*	i. 17. *vivere debet* iustus ex fide	iust. autem ex f. vivit
	iii. 4. *Deus enim verax omnis autem homo mendax*	est autem Deus

Reference and text	Variants (right)	Variants (left)
iv. 5. *credenti* in eum qui iustificat impium *deputatur* fides eius ad iustitiam	credenti + autem reputatur	
v. 5. *Caritas* ½ (dilectio ½) Dei *diffusa* est in cordibus nostris per spiritum sanctum qui datus est nobis	quia dilectio	quia dilectio *Cypr.* q. caritas *m* infusa *Cypr.*
vi. 9. Mors *ei ultra* non dominabitur	illi	in eum jam *m*
vi. 22, 23. *condelector* legi Dei secundum interiorem hominem *sed video* aliam legem in membris meis repugnantem legi mentis meae	condelector + enim video autem	
viii. 7. *Prudentia* carnis inimica est *in Deum*, legi *enim* Dei non est subiecta, *nec* enim potest	sapientia Deo	*Felix* caro legi Dei subiecta non est neque *Tyc.*
viii. 10. Si autem Christus in *nobis* corpus quidem mortuum est propter peccatum, spiritus *autem vita est* propter *iustitiam*	vobis est	vero vita propter iustificationem *m*
viii. 30. Quos autem praedestinavit *illos* et vocavit	vero vivit iustificationem	
x. 10. Sic enim corde credimus ad iustitiam sic ore confessionem facimus ad salutem	hos corde enim creditur...ore autem confessio fit	

AFRICAN LATIN	AUGUSTINE	VULGATE
	ROMANS	
	xii. 3. ...non plus sapere quam oportet sapere, sed sapere ad temperantiam unicuique sicut Deus *partitus est* mensuram fidei	sobrietatem et divisit
m	xiv. 20. malum est homini qui per *offensionem* manducat	offendiculum
	1 CORINTHIANS	
m	ii. 12. Nos autem non spiritum huius mundi accepimus sed spiritum qui ex Deo est, ut sciamus quae a Deo donata sunt nobis	
m	iii. 17. Templum enim Dei sanctum est quod estis vos	
inluminabit consilia cordis *m*	iv. 5. *manifestabit cogitationes cordis* et tunc laus erit unicuique a Deo	consilia cordium
potest dicere Dominum Iesum *Tyc. m* Christum Dom. Iesum *m* ½	xii. 3. Nemo *dicit Dominus Iesus* nisi in spiritu sancto	potest dicere
divisiones autem *n* divisiones autem charismatum *Tyc.*	xii. 4. divisiones *donationum* sunt idem autem spiritus	vero gratiarum

xiii. 1. si linguis hominum loquar et angelorum fio aeramentum sonans et cymbalum tinniens:

xiii. 2. etsi habuero prophetiam et sciero omnia sacramenta et omnem scientiam et habuero omnem fidem ut montes transferam, nihil sum:

xiii. 3. etsi distribuero omnem substantiam meam et tradidero corpus meum ut ardeam, nihil mihi prodest

xv. 10. plus omnibus laboravi non autem (ego) sed gratia Dei (mecum)

xv. 21. per hominem quippe mors et per hominem resurrectio mortuorum

xv. 22. sicut enim in Adam omnes moriuntur, sic in Christo omnes vivificabuntur

xv. 23. Initium Christus deinde qui sunt Christi in praesentia eius: deinde finis cum tradiderit regnum Deo et patri

---

angelorum + caritatem autem non habeam factus sum velut aes aut

noverim; mysteria omnia et + si ita ut transferam + caritatem autem non habuero

d. + in cibos pauperum omnes facultates meas et + si ita ut ardeam + caritatem autem non habuero abundantius + illis

quoniam quidem *om* quippe

et sicut ita et

primitiae deinde + ii Christi + qui in adventu eius crediderunt

---

aut *m* angelorum + caritatem (agapen *Cypr.* ½) autem non habeam (haberem *Cypr.*) *et in vv.* 2, 3 *m Cypr.* unum sum ut *m* aut *m* habeam *m* noverim mysteria omnia *m*

et + si *m Cypr. om* omnem *Cypr.* ita ut *m Cypr.*

om et *m* erogavero *m* in cibos distribuero omnia mea *Cypr.* meam + pauperibus *m* et + si *m Cypr.* proficio *Cypr.*

Nam quia per *m om* quippe *m*

ita *m*

deinde + hi *m* Christi + qui in adventum eius crediderunt *m*

AFRICAN LATIN	AUGUSTINE	VULGATE
	1 CORINTHIANS	
	xv. 28. *ita Deus erit* omnia in omnibus	ut sit Deus
om est enim *m* et alia *m* om enim *Cypr.* a *Cypr.* claritate *m Cypr.* ita *m Cypr.*	xv. 41. Alia *est enim gloria* solis, alia gloria lunae, *alia* gloria stellarum; stella *enim ab* stella differt in *gloria*	om est enim claritas 3 et alia a claritate
	xv. 42. *sic et* resurrectio mortuorum	
	2 CORINTHIANS	
a Deo hab. domum *m* factam *m* ½	v. 1. aedificationem *habemus ex Deo* domum non *manufactam* aeternam in caelis	ex Deo habemus
	v. 6. *Quamdiu enim* sumus in corpore peregrinamur a Domino;	quoniam dum
	v. 7. per fidem enim ambulamus *non* per speciem	et non
	GALATIANS	
suo *Cypr. m*	vi. 9. non deficiamus, tempore enim *proprio* metemus	suo

EPHESIANS

i. 4.	Elegit *nos* ante mundi con-stitutionem	nos + in ipso	
ii. 14.	Ipse *est enim* pax nostra, qui fecit utraque unum	enim est	
v. 8.	*fuistis* enim aliquando tene-brae, nunc autem lux in Domino	eratis	
vi. 12.	Non est *nobis colluctatio adversus* carnem et sanguinem, sed adversus *principes et rectores mundi* tenebrarum harum	principes et potestates adversus mundi rectores	vobis *m* pugna adversum *Tyc.* ad *Cypr.* ½ potestates et principes huius mundi et harum tenebrarum *Cypr.* potestates adversus huius mundi rectores *m*

PHILIPPIANS

ii. 7.	non rapinam arbitratus est esse *aequalis* Deo	se aequalem	se aequalem *Cypr. m*
ii. 7.	*semetipsum exinanivit* formam servi accipiens		*m* se *Cypr.* ½ inanivit *Cypr.* ½
ii. 12.	cum *timore* et tremore	metu	

COLOSSIANS

i. 13.	gratias...Deo...qui *eruit* nos de potestate tenebrarum et trans-tulit in regnum filii *caritatis* suae	eripuit	eripuit *m*
		dilectionis	claritatis *m*

AFRICAN LATIN	AUGUSTINE	VULGATE
	COLOSSIANS	
caelo throni *m*	i. 16. in *caelis sedes* dominationes principatus potestates	throni
ipso habitat *Cypr.*	ii. 9. quia in *illo inhabitat* omnis plenitudo *divinitatis*	ipso divinitatis + corporaliter
	1 TIMOTHY	
m	ii. 5. ...mediator Dei et hominum homo Christus Iesus	
	iii. 16. *Hoc est enim magnum* pietatis sacramentum quod manifestatum est in carne, iustificatum est in spiritu, apparuit angelis, praedicatum est *in* gentibus, creditum est in mundo, assumptum est in gloria	et manifeste magnum est *om* in
	iv. 4. *Omnis* creatura Dei bona est, et nihil *abiciendum* quod cum gratiarum actione *accipitur*	quia omnis reiciendum percipitur
	TITUS	
Deum scire confit. *Tyc.* Deum se scire profitentur operibus autem negant *Faustus*	i. 16. *Confitentur enim se nosse Deum, factis* autem negant	*om* enim

HEBREWS

(r)	xi. 1. Est autem fides *sperantium* substantia, *convictio rerum quae non videntur*	sperandarum substantia rerum argumentum non apparentium

1 JOHN

suffragatorem *Cypr.* ⅗	ii. 1. *Advocatum* habemus *ad* patrem Iesum Christum iustum	apud
apud *h Cypr.*	ii. 16. ...non est *a* patre	ex
ex *h*	ii. 18. *Filioli* novissima hora est	
pueri *h*		

JAMES

	iv. 3. Petitis et non accipitis eo quod male petatis ut in concupiscentiis vestris insumatis	quicunque+ergo
	iv. 4. *Quicunque* voluerit amicus esse saeculi huius inimicus Dei *constituetur*	constituitur

TEXT AND TRANSLATION.

TRACTATUS LXVII.

De eo quod Dominus dicit : *Non turbetur cor vestrum,* usque
ad id : *Iterum venio, accipiam vos ad me ipsum* (Ioan.
xiv. 1—3).

1.   Erigenda est nobis, fratres, ad Deum major intentio,
ut verba sancti Evangelii, quae modo in nostris auribus
sonuerunt, etiam mente capere utcunque possimus.   Ait enim
Dominus Iesus : *Non turbetur cor vestrum, credite* in Deum,
et in me credite.*   Ne mortem tamquam homines timerent, et
ideo turbarentur, consolatur eos, etiam se Deum esse con-
testans.   *Credite,* inquit, *in Deum, et in me credite.*   Consequens est enim, ut si in Deum creditis, et in me credere
debeatis : quod non esset consequens, si Christus non esset
Deus.   *Credite in Deum, et in* eum *credite,* cui natura est,
non rapina, esse aequalem Deo : semetipsum enim exinanivit ;
non tamen formam Dei amittens, sed formam servi accipiens
(Phil. ii. 6, 7).   Mortem metuitis huic formae servi ?   *Non
turbetur cor vestrum,* suscitabit illam forma Dei.

2.   Sed quid est quod sequitur : *In domo Patris mei
mansiones multae sunt,* nisi quia et sibi metuebant ?   Unde
audire debuerunt : *Non turbetur cor vestrum.*   Quis enim
eorum non metueret, cum Petro dictum esset fidentiori

* pauciores MSS. *creditis.*

HOMILY LXVII.

From the Lord's words, *Let not your heart be troubled*, as
far as, *I come again and will receive you unto Myself*
(Jn. xiv. 1—3).

1.   We have need, brethren, to lift up our hearts to God
with more than usual attention, if we are to find the power,
not only of hearing, but also in some measure of apprehending,
the words of the Holy Gospel which have just sounded in our
ears.   For the Lord Jesus says: *Let not your heart be
troubled, believe in God, believe also in Me*.   Being men, the
mention of death was likely to terrify and so trouble them;
therefore He comforts them by the further affirmation that
He is God.   *Believe in God*, He says, *believe also in Me*.   For
it must follow that, if ye believe in God, ye ought to believe
also in Me: it would not so follow, if Christ were not God.
Believe in God, believe also in Him, who, not by usurpation
but by right of nature, is equal with God; for He emptied
Himself, not indeed by surrendering the form of God, but by
taking the form of a servant (Phil. ii. 6, 7).   Do ye fear death
for this form of a servant?   *Let not your heart be troubled*, the
form of a servant shall be raised to life by the form of God.

2.   But why were the next words spoken: *In my Father's
house are many mansions*, but because they were also fearful
for themselves?   This is why He had to say to them: *Let
not your heart be troubled*.   For which of them would not be
fearful, after that Peter, the boldest and most zealous of them,

atque promptiori : *Non cantabit gallus donec ter me neges*
(Ioan. xiii. 38) ? Tamquam ergo essent ab illo perituri, merito
turbabantur ; sed cum audiunt : *In domo Patris mei mansiones multae sunt : si quo minus, dixissem vobis quia vado
parare vobis locum :* a perturbatione recreantur, certi ac fidentes
etiam post pericula tentationum se apud Deum cum Christo
esse mansuros. Quia etsi alius est alio fortior, alius alio
sapientior, alius alio iustior, alius alio sanctior, *in domo Patris
mansiones multae sunt ;* nullus eorum alienabitur ab illa domo,
ubi mansionem pro suo quisque accepturus est merito.
Denarius quidem ille aequalis est omnibus, quem paterfamilias
eis qui operati sunt in vinea iubet dari omnibus, non in eo
discernens qui minus et qui amplius laborarunt (Matth. xx. 9) :
quo utique denario vita significatur aeterna, ubi amplius alio
nemo vivit, quoniam vivendi non est diversa in aeternitate
mensura. Sed multae mansiones diversas meritorum in una
vita aeterna significant dignitates. *Alia est enim gloria solis,
alia gloria lunae, alia gloria stellarum : stella enim ab stella
differt in gloria ; sic et resurrectio mortuorum* (1 Cor. xv. 41).
Tamquam stellae sancti diversas mansiones diversae claritatis,
tamquam in caelo, sortiuntur in regno ; sed propter unum
denarium nullus separatur a regno : atque ita Deus erit omnia
in omnibus (ib. xv. 28), ut, quoniam Deus caritas est, per
caritatem fiat, ut quod habent singuli, commune sit omnibus.
Sic enim quisque etiam ipse habet, cum amat in altero quod
ipse non habet. Non erit itaque aliqua invidia imparis claritatis, quoniam regnabit in omnibus unitas caritatis.

3. Proinde respuendi sunt a corde christiano, qui putant
ideo dictum multas esse mansiones, quia extra regnum caelorum erit aliquid, ubi maneant beati innocentes, qui sine

had been told : *The cock shall not crow, till thou hast denied Me thrice* (Jn. xiii. 38) ? They were naturally troubled, for they feared they were about to perish from Him ; but upon hearing, *in My Father's house are many mansions: if it were not so, I would have told you that I go to prepare a place for you,* they are raised from their distress, in sure and certain hope that, notwithstanding the dangers and temptations that lay before them, there was a home in store for them with Christ in the house of God. For although one man is bolder than another, another wiser, another juster, another holier, yet *in My Father's house are many mansions;* no one of them shall be removed from that house, wherein each is to obtain a dwelling after his deserts. The penny no doubt which the householder bids be given to all those who wrought in his vineyard (Mt. xx. 9) is the same for all ; in respect of it he makes no difference between who laboured less, who more ; and it of course signifies eternal life, where none lives longer than another, for there are no varying measures of life in eternity. The many mansions on the other hand mean varying degrees of dignity in the one eternal life. *For there is one glory of the sun, another glory of the moon, another glory of the stars ; for as star differs from star in glory, so also is the resurrection of the dead* (1 Cor. xv. 41). Like the stars in the sky, the saints in the kingdom have various mansions of varying glory allotted them ; but because the penny is the same for all, none is dissevered from the kingdom, and so completely will God be all in all (ib. xv. 28), that, since God is love, love shall bring it to pass that what each has shall be the common property of all. For when a man loves to see his neighbour in possession of some thing that he lacks himself, he then possesses it himself. Thus there will be no carping at inequality of glory, for unity of love shall reign in all.

3. They therefore are to be rejected with loathing by the Christian soul who take these words about the many mansions to mean that there will be some state outside the kingdom

baptismo ex hac vita emigrarunt, quia sine illo in regnum
caelorum intrare non poterunt. Haec fides non est fides,
quoniam non est vera et catholica fides. Itane tandem stulti
homines et carnalibus cogitationibus excaecati, cum reprobandi
essetis, si mansionem, non dico Petri et Pauli vel cuiuslibet
apostolorum, sed cuiuscunque parvuli baptizati a regno caelorum separaretis ; non vos putatis esse reprobandos, qui domum
Dei Patris inde separatis? Non enim ait Dominus : In
universo mundo, aut in universa creatura, aut in vita vel
beatitudine sempiterna mansiones multae sunt ; sed *in domo*,
inquit, *Patris mei mansiones multae sunt.* Nonne ista est
domus ubi *aedificationem habemus ex Deo, domum non manu-
factam aeternam in caelis* (2 Cor. v. 1)? Nonne ista est
domus de qua cantamus Domino : *Beati qui habitant in
domo tua, in secula seculorum laudabunt te* (Psal. lxxxiii. 5)?
Ergone vos non domum cuiusque baptizati fratris, sed Domum
ipsius Dei Patris, cui omnes fratres dicimus : *Pater noster qui
es in caelis* (Matth. vi. 9), a regno separare caelorum, aut eam
sic dividere audebitis, ut aliquae mansiones ejus sint in regno
caelorum, aliquae autem extra regnum caelorum ? Absit, absit,
ut qui volunt habitare in regno caelorum, in hac stultitia
velint habitare vobiscum ; absit, inquam, ut cum omnis domus
regnantium filiorum non sit alibi nisi in regno, ipsius regiae
domus pars aliqua non sit in regno.

4. *Et si abiero*, inquit, *et praeparavero vobis locum,
iterum venio et accipiam vos ad me ipsum, ut ubi sum ego et
vos sitis. Et quo ego vado scitis, et viam scitis.* O Domine
Iesu, quomodo vadis parare locum, si iam multae mansiones
sunt in domo Patris tui, ubi tecum habitabunt tui ? Aut si
accipis eos ad te ipsum, quomodo iterum venis qui non

of heaven where the innocents, who have departed this life
without baptism, may dwell in blessedness, since without
baptism they can never enter the kingdom. Such a faith is
not the true and catholic faith, and so no faith at all. Are
ye then men so foolish and so utterly blinded by carnal
imaginations—ye who would be condemned if ye sundered
from the kingdom of heaven, I do not say the dwelling-place
of Peter or Paul or of any apostle, but that of even the least
baptized infant—think ye to escape condemnation if ye sunder
from it the house of God the Father? For the Lord does not
say "in the whole world," or "in the whole creation," or "in
everlasting life or bliss are many mansions," but, *in My
Father's house are many mansions.* Is not this the house in
which *we have a building from God, a house not made with
hands, eternal in the heavens* (2 Cor. v. 1)? Is not this the
house concerning which we sing unto the Lord, *Blessed are
they who dwell in Thy house, they will be alway praising
Thee* (Ps. lxxxiv. 4)? Will ye then dare dissever from the
kingdom of heaven, not the house of any baptized brother,
but the house of God the Father Himself, whom all we that
are brethren call *Our Father which art in heaven* (Mt. vi. 9);
or will ye dare so divide up that house that some of its
mansions shall be within the kingdom, and some without? God
forbid, God forbid that they who wish to dwell in the kingdom
of heaven, should wish, while still sunk in such folly as this, to
dwell with you. God forbid, I say, that, while every house of
every son who has come to his throne cannot but be in the
kingdom, any part of the royal house itself should not be there.

4. *And if I go away*, He says, *and provide a place for
you, I come again and will receive you to Myself, that where I
am, ye may be also. And whither I go ye know, and the way
ye know.* O Lord Jesus, how goest Thou to prepare a place,
if there are already many mansions in Thy Father's house
where Thine own shall dwell with Thee? Or how comest
Thou again, if Thou dost never leave them, but dost receive

recedis? Ista, carissimi, si breviter explicare conemur,
quantum videtur hodierno satis esse sermoni, coarctata utique
non clarebunt; et erit ipsa brevitas altera obscuritas; proinde
hoc debitum differamus, quod opportunius vobis patrefamilias
nostro largiente reddamus.

TRACTATUS LXVIII.

In eandem lectionem (xiv. 1—3).

1. Deberi vobis, fratres carissimi, iamque esse red-
dendum quod distuleramus, agnoscimus, quomodo intelligi
possint non esse inter se ista duo contraria, quod cum
dixisset Dominus, *in domo Patris mei mansiones multae sunt:
si quo minus, dixissem vobis quia vado parare vobis locum;*
ubi satis ostendit, ideo se hoc illis dixisse, quia iam ibi sunt
mansiones multae, et non est opus aliquam praeparare; rursus
dicit: *Et si abiero et praeparavero vobis locum, iterum venio
et accipiam vos ad me ipsum, ut ubi ego sum et vos sitis.*
Quomodo vadit et parat locum, si iam multae mansiones
sunt? Si quo minus, dixisset, *vado parare.* Aut si adhuc
parandus est, cur non merito dixisset, *vado parare?* An
istae mansiones et sunt et parandae sunt? Si quo minus
enim essent, dixisset *vado parare.* Et tamen quia ita sunt ut
parandae sint, non eas vadit parare sicut sunt: sed si abierit

them unto Thee? If we try to explain all these things
shortly, dearly beloved, in the space at our disposal in to-day's
discourse, they will surely suffer in clearness from compression, and brevity will prove but fresh obscurity; so let us
postpone the debt and pay it to you at a more convenient
season as the Head of our Household shall vouchsafe us
opportunity.

HOMILY LXVIII.

On the same lection (xiv. 1—3).

1. We admit, beloved brethren, that you have a debt
against us, and that the time has come to pay you what we
had deferred, I mean the explanation how these two statements
may be understood to be not contradictory; that whereas the
Lord had said: *In My Father's house are many mansions; if it
were not so, I would have told you that I go to prepare a place
for you* (whereby He clearly shewed that He had said this to
them just because there are already many mansions there and
so no need of providing any), He then saith on the other
hand: *And if I go and provide a place for you, I come again
and will receive you unto Myself, that where I am there ye
may be also.* How can He go and prepare a place, if there
are already many mansions? If it were not so, He would
have said, *I go to prepare.* Or if the place still needed to be
prepared, why should He not have said with perfect propriety,
I go to prepare it? Can it be that those mansions in one
sense are in existence, in another have yet to be prepared?
For if they had not been in existence, He would have said,
I go to prepare them. And yet, because their present state is
such that they still need to be prepared, He does not go to
prepare them in the sense in which they already are; but if

et paraverit sicut futurae sunt, iterum veniens accipiet suos ad se ipsum, ut ubi est ipse sint etiam ipsi. Quomodo ergo mansiones in domo Patris non aliae, sed ipsae, et sine dubio iam sunt sicut parandae non sunt, et nondum sunt sicut parandae sunt? Quomodo putamus, nisi quomodo etiam propheta praedicat Deum, quia *fecit quae futura sunt* (Isai. xlv. 11)? Non enim ait: Qui facturus est quae futura sunt; sed, *qui fecit quae futura sunt*. Ergo et fecit ea, et facturus est ea. Nam neque facta sunt, si ipse non fecit: neque futura sunt, si ipse non fecerit. Fecit ergo ea praedestinando, facturus est operando. Sicut discipulos quando elegerit, satis indicat Evangelium, tunc utique quando eos vocavit: et tamen ait Apostolus: *Elegit nos ante mundi constitutionem* (Ephes. i. 4): praedestinando utique, non vocando. *Quos autem praedestinavit, illos et vocavit* (Rom. viii. 30); elegit praedestinando ante mundi constitutionem, elegit vocando ante mundi consummationem. Sic et mansiones praeparavit et praeparat; nec alias, sed quas praeparavit, has praeparat, *qui fecit quae futura sunt:* quas praeparavit praedestinando, praeparat operando. Iam ergo sunt in praedestinatione: si quo minus, dixisset, ibo et parabo, id est, praedestinabo. Sed quia nondum sunt in operatione, *et si abiero*, inquit, *et praeparavero vobis locum, iterum venio et accipiam vos ad me ipsum.*

He goes and prepares them in the sense in which they are to be, He will on His coming again receive His own to Himself, that where He is, they may also be. How then can it be said of one and the same set of mansions in the Father's House, that at this moment they exist in a sense which precludes the necessity of preparing them, and at the same time that they do not yet exist in the sense in which they must be prepared? How else indeed but in the sense in which the prophet speaks of God as having already *made things which are yet to be* (Is. xlv. 11)? For he does not say, "who is about to make things which are to be," but, *who hath made things which are yet to be.* So in one sense He has made them, and in another sense He is going to make them. For it is not true either that they have been made, except so far as He has made them; or that they are going to be, except so far as He shall make them. So then He has made them by predestination; He is going to make them by actual realization.

Similarly the Gospel clearly shews that the moment of His choosing the disciples was precisely that in which He called them; and yet the Apostle says, *He chose us before the foundation of the world* (Eph. i. 4)—plainly, chose by pre-destining, not by calling us. *But whom He predestinated, them He also called* (Rom. viii. 30): He chose them by pre-destinating them before the world's beginning, He chose them by calling them before its close. So also those mansions He has provided and is providing; not different ones, but those which He has already provided is He now providing, *who hath made things which are yet to be;* mansions which He has provided by predestination, He is providing by actual realiza-tion. Thus they already exist in God's predestination; else He would have said "I will go and will prepare them," that is, "I will predestinate." But because they are not yet in actual realization He says, *And if I go away and pro-vide a place for you, I come again and will receive you unto Myself.*

2.   Parat autem quodam modo mansiones, mansionibus
parando mansores.   Quippe cum dixerit, *in domo Patris mei
mansiones multae sunt ;* quid putamus esse domum Dei, nisi
templum Dei ?   Quod autem sit, interrogetur Apostolus et
respondeat :   *Templum enim Dei sanctum est, quod estis vos*
(1 Cor. iii. 17).   Hoc est etiam regnum Dei, quod Filius
traditurus est Patri : unde dicit idem Apostolus : *Initium
Christus, deinde qui sunt Christi in praesentia ejus : deinde
finis, cum tradiderit regnum Deo et Patri* (1 Cor. xv. 23, 24) :
id est, quos redemit sanguine suo, tradiderit contemplando
etiam Patri suo.   Hoc est regnum caelorum de quo dicitur :
*Simile est regnum caelorum homini seminanti bonum semen in
agro suo.   Bonum autem semen, hi sunt filii regni :* qui etsi
nunc habent permixta zizania, *mittet* in fine Rex ipse *angelos
suos, et colligent de regno ejus omnia scandala.   Tunc iusti
fulgebunt sicut sol, in regno Patris sui* (Matth. xiii. 24, 38—43).
Regnum fulgebit in regno, cum regno venerit regnum, quod
nunc oramus et dicimus : *Veniat regnum tuum* (ib. vi. 10).
Nunc ergo iam regnum vocatur, sed adhuc convocatur :
si enim regnum non vocaretur, *colligent de regno ejus omnia
scandala*, non diceretur.   Sed nondum regnat hoc regnum.
Proinde sic iam est regnum ut, cum de illo collecta fuerint
omnia scandala, tunc perveniat ad regnum : ut non solum
regni nomen, sed etiam regnandi habeat potestatem.   Huic
quippe regno ad dexteram stanti in fine dicetur : *Venite,
benedicti Patris mei, percipite regnum* (Matth. xxv. 34) : id
est, qui regnum eratis et non regnabatis, venite, regnate : ut
quod in spe fueratis, etiam in re esse possitis.   Haec ergo
domus Dei, hoc templum Dei, hoc regnum Dei regnumque

2. Now He prepares the mansions in a certain sense by preparing occupants for them. For surely when He says, *in My Father's house are many mansions*, we must understand the house of God to be naught other than the temple of God. And what that is, ask the Apostle and hear him answer: *For the temple of God is holy, which temple are ye* (1 Cor. iii. 17). Likewise it is the kingdom of God, which the Son is to deliver up to the Father; whence the same Apostle says, *Christ the beginning, then they that are Christ's in His appearing: then the end, when He shall have delivered up the kingdom to God, even the Father* (1 Cor. xv. 23, 24); that is, delivered up those whom He hath purchased with His blood to gaze upon His Father also. This is that kingdom of heaven of which it is said, *The kingdom of heaven is like unto a man sowing good seed in his field. Now the good seed is the children of the kingdom*, and though now they are mixed with tares, the king in the end *will* Himself *send His angels and they shall gather out of His kingdom all things that offend. Then shall the righteous shine forth as the sun in the kingdom of their Father* (Mt. xiii. 24, 38—43). The kingdom shall shine forth in the kingdom, when the kingdom comes to its kingdom, even as now we pray, saying, *Thy kingdom come* (ib. vi. 10). Therefore though it is even now called a kingdom, it is still only being called together; for if it were not called a kingdom, it would not be said, *they shall gather all things that offend out of His kingdom.* But this kingdom hath not yet its full kingly state. Hence it is to-day a kingdom in the sense that, when out of it have been gathered all offences, it then shall reach a kingly state; that it may enjoy not only the royal name but royal power. Yea, to this kingdom, standing at His right hand, it will be said at the last, *Come, ye blessed of My Father, receive the kingdom* (Mt. xxv. 34); come, ye who were a kingdom but did not reign as kings, come, reign; that ye may now become in fact that which ye were of old in hope. So then this house of God, this temple of God, this kingdom

caelorum adhuc aedificatur, adhuc fabricatur, adhuc paratur,
adhuc congregatur.   In illo erunt mansiones, sicut eas adhuc
parat Dominus : in illo iam sunt, sicut praedestinavit iam
Dominus.

3.   Sed quid est quod ut praepararet abiit, cum profecto
nos ipsos praepararet, quod non faciet si reliquerit ?   Agnosco,
Domine, ut possum : nimirum illud significas, quia ut parentur
istae mansiones, vivere debet *iustus ex fide* (Rom. i. 17).
Qui enim a Domino peregrinatur, opus habet ex fide vivere ;
quia per hanc ad speciem contemplandam paratur.   *Beati*
enim *mundo corde, quia ipsi Deum videbunt* (Matth. v. 8) : et,
Fide mundat corda eorum (Act. xv. 9).   Illud in Evangelio,
hoc in apostolorum Actibus legitur.   Fides autem, qua eorum
qui Deum visuri sunt, quamdiu peregrinantur, corda mundantur, quod non videt credit : nam si vides, non est fides.
Credenti colligitur meritum, videnti redditur praemium.   Eat
ergo Dominus et paret locum ; eat ne videatur, lateat ut
credatur.   Tunc enim locus paratur, si ex fide vivatur.   Creditus
desideretur, ut desideratus habeatur : desiderium dilectionis,
praeparatio est mansionis.   Ita, Domine, para quod paras : nos
enim tibi paras, et te nobis paras ; quoniam locum paras, et
tibi in nobis, et in te nobis.   Tu enim dixisti : *Manete in me, et
ego in vobis* (Ioan. xv. 4).   Quantum quisque fuerit particeps
tui, alius minus, alius amplius, haec erit diversitas praemiorum
pro diversitate meritorum : haec erit multitudo mansionum
pro disparilitate mansorum ; sed tamen omnium in aeternitate
vivorum et sine fine beatorum.   Quid est quod vadis ?   Quid
est quod venis ?   Si bene te intelligo, nec unde vadis, nec

of God and kingdom of heaven, is still in building, still in fashioning, still in preparation, still in gathering. In it there will be mansions as the Lord is still preparing them; in it there are already mansions as the Lord hath foreordained them.

3. But how can it be that He went away to make preparation, since assuredly it is ourselves that He was to provide and this He will never do if He desert us? I take Thy meaning, Lord, as best I may; Thou surely meanest by this, that for the due preparation of those mansions, *the just must live by faith* (Rom. i. 17). For he that is absent from the Lord must live by faith; because through this he is prepared to look upon His Face. For *blessed are the pure in heart, for they shall see God* (Mt. v. 8); and, *by faith He purifies their hearts* (Acts xv. 9). The former text is in the Gospel, the latter in the Acts of the Apostles. Now faith, by which the hearts of those are cleansed who shall see God even while they are absent from Him, believes that which it sees not; for seeing is not believing. Faith earns the blessing, sight reaps the reward. So let the Lord go and prepare a place; go, that He be not seen; hide Himself, that He may be believed. The place *is* being prepared, if we live by faith.

Let belief in it beget longing love for it, that love may win possession. Love's longing is the dwelling's preparation. Go then, Lord, prepare what Thou preparest; for Thou preparest us for Thee and Thyself for us; Thou preparest a place both for Thyself in us, and for us in Thyself. For Thou hast said, *Abide in me, and I in you* (Jn. xv. 4). As each one's share in Thee hath varied, some having more, some less, so the reward shall vary, answering to the varying desert of each; thus the number of the dwellings shall be many to suit the inequality of the inmates, who, nevertheless, all alike enjoy eternity of life and endless bliss. What meaneth it that Thou goest? What, that Thou comest? If I understand Thee right, Thou withdrawest neither from the place from which Thou goest from us, nor from that from which

unde venis, recedis : vadis latendo, venis apparendo. Sed
nisi maneas regendo, ut proficiamus bene vivendo ; quomodo
parabitur locus, ubi possimus manere perfruendo ? Haec de
verbis quae recitata sunt evangelicis, satis dicta sint, quous-
que ait Dominus : *Iterum venio et accipiam vos ad me ipsum.*
Quid autem sit quod sequitur, *ut ubi ego sum, et vos sitis :*
et quo ego vado scitis, et viam scitis (Ioan. xiv. 3, 4) ; post
interrogationem quae sequitur a discipulo factam, tamquam
per eum et nos interrogemus, melius audiemus opportuniusque
tractabimus.

TRACTATUS LXIX.

In id quod Dominus dicit : *Et quo ego vado scitis, et viam*
　　　scitis : usque ad id : *Nemo venit ad Patrem nisi per me*
　　　(xiv. 4—6).

1.　Nunc est, dilectissimi, ut quantum valemus, intelligamus de verbis Domini posterioribus priora et consequentibus
praecedentia, in eo quod audistis apostolo Thomae interroganti
esse responsum. Dixerat enim superius Dominus, cum de
mansionibus loqueretur, quas et esse dixit in domo Patris sui,
et ire se ut praepararet eas ; ubi intelleximus et esse iam
mansiones ipsas in praedestinatione, et praeparari eas, cum
eorum qui ibi mansuri sunt per fidem corda mundantur, quoniam
ipsa Dei domus ipsi sunt : et quid est aliud manere in domo
Dei, quam esse in populo Dei, cum idem populus est in Deo
et Deus in eo ? hoc ut praepararet, Dominus abiit ; ut

Thou comest to us. Thou goest by concealing, and comest by revealing Thyself. But unless Thou abide with us by ruling us so that we advance by well-doing, how shall there be a place prepared for us to dwell in and enjoy?

Let what has been said suffice for what we have heard read from the Gospel record as far as where the Lord says, *I come again, and will receive you unto Myself.* But the meaning of the next words, *that where I am, there ye may be also; and whither I go ye know, and the way ye know* (Jn. xiv. 3, 4), that we shall be in better mood to hear and in better position to handle, when the question following has been asked by the disciple, whose enquiry we may take to express our own.

HOMILY LXIX.

On the Lord's words, *And whither I go ye know, and the way ye know,* as far as, *No man cometh unto the Father but by Me* (xiv. 4—6).

1. Our present duty, my beloved, is to try to understand, as best we can, the Lord's earlier from His later utterance, His previous words from those that follow, in the reply which ye heard given to the Apostle Thomas when he asked his question. For the Lord had said above, when speaking of the mansions which He said were already in His Father's house, which yet He was going to provide, whereby we learnt both that those very mansions already exist in God's predestination and also are being provided by the cleansing through faith of the hearts of those who are to dwell therein, because they are themselves the very house of God—and what else is dwelling in the house of God but belonging to God's people, since His people are in God and God in them? It was to provide this that the Lord went hence, that by

credendo in eum qui non videtur, ea quae in specie semper
futura est, nunc per fidem mansio praeparetur : propter hoc
ergo dixerat : *Et si abiero et praeparavero vobis locum, iterum
venio et accipiam vos ad me ipsum, ut ubi ego sum et vos sitis :
et quo ego vado scitis et viam scitis.*   Ad haec *dicit ei Thomas:
Domine, nescimus quo vadis, et quomodo possumus viam scire?*
Utrumque illos Dominus dixerat scire, utrumque dicit iste
nescire, et locum quo itur, et viam qua itur.   Sed nescit ille
mentiri : ergo isti sciebant, et scire se nesciebant.   Con-
vincat eos iam scire, quod se putant adhuc usque nescire.
Dicit ei Iesus: Ego sum via, et veritas, et vita.   Quid est,
fratres ?   Ecce audivimus discipulum interrogantem, audivimus
et Magistrum docentem : et nondum capimus, etiam post
vocem sonantem, sententiam latitantem.   Sed quid non possumus capere ?   Numquid poterant ei dicere apostoli eius cum
quibus loquebatur : Nescimus te ?   Proinde si eum sciebant,
et via ipse est, viam sciebant ; si eum sciebant, et veritas ipse
est, veritatem sciebant ; si eum sciebant, et vita ipse est,
vitam sciebant.   Ecce scire convicti sunt, quod se scire
nesciebant.

    2.   Quid igitur et nos in isto sermone non cepimus ?   Quid
putatis, fratres mei, nisi quia dixit : *Et quo vado scitis, et
viam scitis?*   Et ecce cognovimus quod sciebant viam, quia
sciebant ipsum qui est via ; sed via est qua itur ; numquid via
est et quo itur ?   Utrumque autem illos dixerat scire, et quo
vadit et viam.   Opus ergo erat, ut diceret, *Ego sum via,* ut
ostenderet eos, quia eum scirent, viam scire quam putaverunt
se nescire ; quid autem opus erat ut diceret, *Ego sum via, et*

faith in Him who is not seen, faith may even now provide the mansion the full vision of which is ever future—therefore He had said, *And if I go away and prepare a place for you, I come again and will receive you unto Myself, that where I am, there ye may be also; and whither I go ye know, and the way ye know.* Upon this, *Thomas saith unto Him, Lord, we know not whither Thou goest, and how can we know the way?* The Lord had said that they knew both, Thomas declares that they know neither—neither the journey's goal nor the way to it. But the Lord cannot lie; they therefore knew, and knew not that they knew. Hear Him prove that they already know that which they think that up to that moment they do not know. *Jesus saith unto him, I am the Way, and the Truth, and the Life.* What is this, my brethren? Lo, we have heard the disciple ask, we have heard the Master teach him; yet, though the voice has sounded in our ears, we do not yet take in the thought that lies concealed. But what is it that we fail to grasp? Could His apostles with whom He was speaking say to Him: "We know Thee not"? Then if they knew Him, and He is the Way, they knew the Way; if they knew Him, and He is the Truth, they knew the Truth; if they knew Him, and He is the Life, they knew the Life. So they stand convinced of knowing what they knew not that they knew.

2. What is it then in that discourse that we as well as they have failed to grasp? What do you think it can be, my brethren, other than the words, *And whither I go ye know, and the way ye know?* And now, look you, we have learned that they knew the way, because they knew Him who is the Way. But the way is that by which we go; is the way also the point to which we move? Now He had said that they knew both—whither He is going and the way. There was need then for Him to say, *I am the Way*, to shew them that, knowing Him, they knew the way they thought they did not know; but what need was there to say, *I am the*

2—2

veritas, et vita, cum via cognita qua iret, restaret nosse quo iret ; nisi quia ibat ad veritatem, ibat ad vitam ? Ibat ergo ad se ipsum per se ipsum. Et nos quo imus, nisi ad ipsum ; et qua imus, nisi per ipsum ? Ipse igitur ad se ipsum per se ipsum ; nos ad ipsum per ipsum : imo vero et ad Patrem et ipse et nos. Nam et de se ipso alibi dicit : *Ad Patrem vado* (Ioan. xvi. 10) ; et hoc loco propter nos, *nemo,* inquit, *venit ad Patrem, nisi per me* (ib. xiv. 6). Ac per hoc et ipse per se ipsum et ad se ipsum et ad Patrem, et nos per ipsum et ad ipsum et ad Patrem. Quis haec capit, nisi qui spiritaliter sapit ? Et quantum est quod hic capit, etiamsi spiritaliter sapit ? Fratres, quid a me ista vobis vultis exponi ? Cogitate quam excelsa sint. Videtis quid sim, video quid sitis : in omnibus nobis *corpus quod corrumpitur aggravat animam, et deprimit terrena inhabitatio sensum multa cogitantem* (Sap. ix. 15). Putamusne possumus dicere : *Ad te levavi animam meam, qui habitas in caelo* (Psal. cxxii. 1) ? Sed sub tanto pondere ubi *ingemiscimus gravati* (2 Cor. v. 4), quomodo levabo animam meam, nisi mecum levet qui posuit pro me suam ? Dicam ergo quod possum, capiat vestrum qui potest. Quo donante dico, eo donante capit qui capit, et eo donante credit qui nondum capit. *Nisi* enim *credideritis,* inquit propheta, *non intelligetis* (Isai. vii. 9).

3. Dic mihi, Domine meus, quid dicam servis tuis con-servis meis ? Thomas apostolus ut te interrogaret, habuit te ante se ; nec tamen intelligeret te, nisi haberet in se ; ego interrogo te, quia te scio esse super me : interrogo autem in quantum possum super me effundere animam meam, ubi non

Way, and the Truth, and the Life, seeing that, now that they
knew the way by which He went, they only had to learn His
goal, if it was not that He was going to the Truth, to the
Life ? He was going therefore to Himself through Himself.
And we, whither do we go except to Him ; and which way go
we save by Him ? He to Himself then goeth through Himself, and we to Him through Him ; nay, rather, to the Father
also go we, both He and we. For concerning Himself He
saith elsewhere, *I go to the Father* (Jn. xvi. 10), and in this
passage for our sake He saith, *No man cometh to the Father
but by Me* (ib. xiv. 6). Accordingly He Himself goeth through
Himself both to Himself and to the Father; and we also through
Him both to Him and to the Father. Who but him that is
spiritually minded receiveth this ? And how much doth even
such an one receive ? Brethren, why would you have me
explain these things to you ? Consider how lofty they are.
Ye see what I am, I see what ye are ; in all of us *a corruptible
body weigheth down the soul, and the earthy habitation lieth
heavy on the mind that museth upon many things* (Wisd.
ix. 15). Do you think we can say, *To Thee have I lifted up
my soul, O Thou that dwellest in the heavens* (Ps. cxxiii. 1) ?
How shall I, oppressed by such a weight, under which *we
groan, being burdened* (2 Cor. v. 4), lift up my soul, unless He
lift it up with me, who for me laid down His own ? Let me
speak then, as best I can ; and let each of you who can, comprehend it. It is by His gift that I speak, by His gift that he
comprehends who does comprehend, and by His gift that he
who does not yet comprehend believes. For, *except ye believe,*
the prophet says, *ye shall not understand* (Is. vii. 9).

3. Tell Thou me, my Lord, what to tell Thy servants and
my fellow-servants. The Apostle Thomas had Thee before
his eyes to question Thee ; yet for all that, he had not understood Thee, had he not had Thee in his heart : I question
Thee, because I know Thee to be high above me ; I question
Thee in so far as I am able to pour out my soul on high

sonantem et tamen docentem audiam te. Dic mihi, obsecro,
quomodo vadis ad te? Numquidnam ut venires ad nos,
reliqueras te: maxime quia non a te ipso venisti, sed Pater
te misit? Scio quidem quod te exinanisti, sed quia formam
servi accepisti (Philip. ii. 7), non quia formam Dei vel ad quam
redires dimisisti, vel quam reciperes amisisti; et tamen venisti,
et non solum usque ad carnales oculos, verum etiam usque ad
manus hominum pervenisti. Quomodo, nisi in carne? Per
hanc venisti manens ubi eras, per hanc rediisti non relinquens
quo veneras. Si ergo per hanc venisti et rediisti, per hanc
procul dubio non solum nobis es qua veniremus ad te, verum
etiam tibi qua venires et redires via fuisti. Cum vero ad
vitam, quod es ipse, iisti, eandem profecto carnem tuam de
morte ad vitam duxisti. Aliud quippe Dei Verbum est, aliud
homo; sed *Verbum caro factum est,* id est homo. Non
itaque alia Verbi, alia est hominis persona, quoniam utrumque
est Christus una persona: ac per hoc quemadmodum caro cum
mortua est, Christus est mortuus; et cum caro sepulta est,
Christus est sepultus: sic enim *corde credimus ad iustitiam,
sic ore confessionem facimus ad salutem* (Rom. x. 10): ita
cum caro a morte venit ad vitam, Christus venit ad vitam.
Et quia Verbum Dei Christus est, Christus est vita. Ita miro
quodam et ineffabili modo, qui nunquam dimisit vel amisit se
ipsum, venit ad se ipsum. Venerat autem, ut dictum est, per
carnem Deus ad homines, veritas ad mendaces : *Deus* enim
verax, omnis autem homo mendax (Rom. iii. 4). Cum itaque
ab hominibus abstulit, atque illuc ubi nemo mentitur, carnem
suam levavit; idem ipse, quia Verbum caro factum est, per se
ipsum, id est, per carnem, ad veritatem, quod est ipse, remeavit.
Quam quidem veritatem, quamvis inter mendaces, et in morte
servavit: aliquando enim Christus fuit mortuus, sed nunquam
fuit falsus.

where, though I may not hear Thee speak, I hear Thee teach. Tell me, I beseech Thee, how goest Thou to Thyself? It cannot be that Thou didst leave Thyself to come to us, for of a truth Thou camest not from Thyself, but the Father sent Thee. I know that Thou didst empty Thyself, but it was by taking the form of a servant (Phil. ii. 7), not by giving up the form of God to return to it again, nor by losing it to receive it back again; and yet Thou didst come not only within the scope of eyes of flesh, but even within the touch of human hands. How, but in the flesh? By means of flesh Thou camest, yet remaining where Thou wast; by the same means Thou didst return, still abiding there whither Thou hadst come. If then by this means Thou didst come and go, by the same means surely not only art Thou the Way for us to come to Thee, but wast also the Way for Thyself to come and to return. And when Thou didst go to Life, which is Thyself, Thou didst raise that same flesh of Thine from death to life. The Word of God indeed is one thing, man another; but *the Word became flesh*, i.e. man. And so there are not two persons, one of the Word and the other of man, for Christ who is but one Person, is both; and therefore just as when the flesh died, Christ died; when the flesh was buried, Christ was buried (for so *we believe with the heart unto righteousness and with the mouth make confession unto salvation*, Rom. x. 10), so when the flesh came to life from death, Christ came to life. And because the Word of God is Christ, Christ is Life. Thus in some marvellous and unspeakable way He, who never gave up or lost Himself, came to Himself. But God, as has been said, had come to men through flesh, the Truth to liars; for *God is true, but every man a liar* (Rom. iii. 4). When then He removed His flesh from men and raised it up to that place where no liar is, He Himself, in that the Word was made flesh, returned through Himself, that is, through flesh, to the Truth, which is Himself; which Truth, albeit among liars, He kept in death itself; for Christ died once, but never was He false.

4. Accipite quamvis diversum et longe impar exemplum, tamen utcunque ad intelligendum Deum, ex his quae propius subjecta sunt Deo. Ecce ego ipse, quantum attinet ad animum meum, cum hoc sim quod estis et vos, si taceo, apud me ipsum sum: si autem loquor vobis quod intelligatis, quodam modo ad vos procedo, nec me relinquo, sed et ad vos accedo, et non recedo unde procedo. Cum autem tacuero, quodam modo ad me redeo; et quodam modo vobiscum maneo, si tenueritis quod audistis in sermone quem dico. Si hoc potest imago quam fecit Deus, quid potest non a Deo facta, sed ex Deo nata imago Dei Deus: cujus illud, quo ad nos egressus est, et in quo a nobis regressus est, corpus, non sicut meus elapsus est sonus, sed manet ibi ubi iam non moritur, et *mors ei ultra non dominabitur* (Rom. vi. 9)? Multa de his evangelicis verbis adhuc dici fortasse poterant et debebant: sed non sunt corda vestra spiritalibus cibis quamlibet suavibus oneranda: maxime quia *spiritus promptus est, caro autem infirma* (Matth. xxvi. 41).

TRACTATUS LXX.

De eo quod Dominus ait: *Si cognovissetis me, et Patrem meum utique cognovissetis*, usque ad id: *Non credis, quia ego in Patre, et Pater in me est?* (xiv. 7—10).

1. Verba sancti Evangelii, fratres, ita recte intelliguntur, si cum superioribus reperiuntur habere concordiam: convenire enim debent praecedentia consequentibus, quando veritas loquitur. Superius dixerat Dominus: *Et si abiero, et prae-*

4. Take an instance, remote indeed and far inferior, yet not unapt to teach us about God, from a sphere of things that touches the divine. Take my own case and the operations of my mind ; being as I am the same as you yourselves, I abide with myself so long as I hold my peace ; but if I speak and make you understand, I do in a certain sense go forth to you without leaving myself, and approach you without quitting the place whence I go forth. And when I cease speaking I return in some sort to myself ; and yet in some sort abide with you, if ye remember what ye heard in my discourse. If the image which God made is capable of this, how much more the image of God not made by God but be-gotten by God, even God's very Self ! since that bodily form by which He came forth to us and in which He went away from us has not, like the sound of my words, passed away, but abideth there where it henceforth dieth no more and *death shall have no more dominion over it* (Rom. vi. 9). I do not doubt that much might and should still be said upon these words of the Gospel ; but your hearts must not be over-charged with spiritual food, however sweet ; the more so as *the spirit is willing, but the flesh is weak* (Mt. xxvi. 41).

HOMILY LXX.

From the Lord's words, *If ye had known Me, ye would surely have known My Father also,* as far as, *Believest thou not that I am in the Father, and the Father in Me?* (xiv. 7—10).

1. We have reached the true meaning of a passage in the Holy Gospel, brethren, when we find that it agrees with previous utterances, for antecedent is bound to match con-clusion when it is the Truth that speaks. Now the Lord had

*paravero vobis locum, iterum venio, et accipiam vos ad me
ipsum, ut ubi ego sum, et vos sitis;* deinde addiderat: *Et quo
ego vado scitis, et viam scitis;* nihilque aliud ostendit esse
quod dixit, nisi quia ipsum sciebant.　Quid ergo esset ire ad
se ipsum per se ipsum, quod etiam discipulis praestat ut eant
ad ipsum per ipsum, ut potuimus pristino sermone iam diximus.
Quod itaque ait: *Ut ubi ego sum, et vos sitis,* ubi erant futuri
nisi in ipso ?　Ac per hoc est etiam ipse in se ipso, et ideo ibi
illi ubi et ipse, id est, in ipso.　Ipse est igitur vita aeterna in
qua futuri sumus, cum acceperit nos ad se : et ipsa vita aeterna
quod ipse est in ipso est, ut ubi est ipse, et nos simus, hoc
est, in ipso.　*Sicut enim habet Pater vitam in semetipso,* et
utique non aliud est vita quam habet, nisi quod est ipse qui
hanc habet: *sic dedit Filio habere vitam in semetipso* (Joan.
v. 26), cum ipse sit eadem vita quam habet in semetipso.
Numquid autem nos vita, quod est ipse, hoc erimus, cum in
illa vita, hoc est in ipso esse coeperimus ?　Non utique, quia
ipse exsistendo vita habet vitam, et ipse est quod habet, et
quod vita est in ipso, ipse est in se ipso : nos autem non ipsa
vita, sed ipsius vitae participes sumus; atque ita ibi erimus, ut
in nobis ipsis non quod ipse est esse possimus, sed nos ipsi non
vita ipsum habeamus vitam, qui se ipsum habet vitam, eo
quod ipse sit vita.　Denique ipse et in se ipso est immutabiliter, et in Patre inseparabiliter: nos vero cum in nobis ipsis
esse voluissemus, ad nos ipsos turbati sumus; unde illa vox
est: *Ad me ipsum turbata est anima mea* (Psal. xli. 7):
atque in deterius commutati, neque id quod fuimus manere
potuimus.　Cum autem per ipsum venimus ad Patrem, sicut
ait: *Nemo venit ad Patrem nisi per me:* manentes in
illo, nec a Patre nos quisquam poterit separare, nec ab
illo.

previously said, *And if I go away, and provide a place for you, I come again, and will receive you unto Myself, that where I am, there ye may be also;* then He had added, *And whither I go ye know, and the way ye know;* and He shewed that the simple meaning of His words was that they knew Him. What He meant then by "going to Himself through Himself" (which thing—coming to Him through Him—He likewise offers His disciples) we explained to you as best we could in the last discourse. And with regard to His words, *that where I am, there ye may be also,* where were they to be except in Him? Consequently both He is in Himself, and they must needs be where He is, that is, in Himself. He therefore is the eternal life which is to be our lot, when He shall have received us unto Himself; and that life eternal which He is, is in Him, that where He is we too may be, that is, in Him. *For as the Father hath life in Himself* and assuredly the life He hath is none other than what He is who hath it; *so hath He given to the Son to have life in Himself* (Jn. v. 26), being Himself the life which He hath in Himself. But shall we be what He is, namely life, when we begin existence in that life, that is, in Him? No indeed, because He, being life, hath life by the mere fact of His existence, and is Himself that which He hath—and life in Him is simply Himself in Himself; but we are not life, but partakers of His life; we shall be in life indeed, but we can never be in ourselves what He is; we who are not life ourselves shall have Him as our life, who hath Himself as life because He is life. Similarly, He is both in Himself unchangeably and in the Father inseparably; but we, whenever we tried to be in ourselves we were troubled at ourselves—whence that cry, *My soul was troubled at myself* (Ps. xlii. 6)—and changing from bad to worse we could not even remain what we were. But when we come to the Father by Him, as He saith, *No man cometh unto the Father but by Me,* by abiding in Him none shall be able to separate us either from the Father or from Him.

2. Connectens itaque consequentia praecedentibus, *Si cognovistis me*, inquit, *et Patrem meum utique cognovistis.* Hoc est quod ait : *Nemo venit ad Patrem nisi per me.* Deinde subiungit: *Et amodo cognoscetis eum, et vidistis eum.* Sed Philippus unus ex apostolis, quid audierit non intelligens, *Domine*, inquit, *ostende nobis Patrem, et sufficit nobis.* Cui Dominus, *Tanto*, inquit, *tempore vobiscum sum, et non cognovistis me, Philippe? Qui videt me, videt et Patrem.* Ecce increpat quod tanto tempore cum ipsis erat, et non cognoscebatur. Nonne ipse dixerat: *Et quo ego vado scitis, et viam scitis:* et se nescire dicentes, eos haec scire convicerat, addendo atque dicendo: *Ego sum via, veritas et vita?* Quomodo nunc dicit: *Tanto tempore vobiscum sum, et non cognovistis me?* cum profecto et quo iret, et viam scirent, non ob aliud nisi quod ipsum utique scirent? Sed facile ista solvitur quaestio, si dicamus, quod eum aliqui eorum sciebant, aliqui nesciebant, atque in his qui nesciebant et Philippus erat; ut quod ait: *Et quo ego vado scitis, et viam scitis*, illis dixisse intelligatur qui sciebant; non Philippo cui dictum est: *Tanto tempore vobiscum sum, et non cognovistis me, Philippe?* His ergo qui Filium iam noverant, etiam illud de Patre dictum est: *Et amodo cognoscetis eum et vidistis eum:* dictum est enim propter omnimodam similitudinem, quae illi cum Patre est, ut ideo amodo dicerentur nosse Patrem, quia noverant similem Filium   Ergo iam sciebant Filium, etsi non omnes, certe quidam eorum quibus dicitur: *Et quo vado scitis, et viam scitis:* ipse est enim via. Sed Patrem nesciebant, ideo audiunt: *Si cognovistis me, et Patrem meum cognovistis:* per

2. So then linking the words which follow with what went before, *If ye have known Me*, He saith, *ye have surely known My Father also.* This is what He means by *No man cometh to the Father but by Me.* Then He adds, *And from henceforth ye shall know Him, and have seen Him.* But saith Philip, one of the Apostles, not understanding what he heard, *Lord, shew us the Father, and it sufficeth us.* To whom the Lord replies, *Have I been so long time with you, and have ye not known Me, Philip? he that seeth Me seeth the Father also.* He is complaining that though He was so long with them, He was yet not known of them. Had He not Himself said, *And whither I go ye know, and the way ye know,* and, when they said they did not know, had proved that they did know, by going on to say, *I am the Way, the Truth and the Life*? How can He now say, *Have I been so long time with you, and have ye not known Me?* when most certainly they knew both whither He was going and the way, for the simple reason that they assuredly knew Him? The question is easily answered if we may say that some of them knew Him and some did not and that Philip was of these last, so that the words, *And whither I go ye know, and the way ye know,* may be understood to be spoken to those that knew, and not to Philip to whom He said, *Have I been so long time with you, and have ye not known Me, Philip?* It is to those then who already knew the Son that the further words concerning the Father were spoken, *And from henceforth ye shall know Him, and have seen Him;* they were spoken because of the perfect likeness which there is between Him and the Father, so that they might henceforth be said to know the Father because they knew the Son who is like Him. Already then some of them at least, though not all, did know the Son; those, I mean, to whom it is said, *And whither I go ye know, and the way ye know;* for He is the Way. But they knew not the Father, and therefore they are told, *If ye have known Me, ye have known My Father also*, yea, known Him through Me. I

me utique et illum. Alius enim ego sum, alius ille. Sed ne
putarent dissimilem, *Et amodo*, inquit, *cognoscetis eum, et
vidistis eum.* Viderunt enim eius simillimum Filium, sed
admonendi fuerant talem esse etiam Patrem quem nondum
videbant, qualis est Filius quem videbant. Et ad hoc valet
quod postea Philippo dicitur: *Qui videt me, videt et Patrem.*
Non quod ipse esset Pater et Filius, quod in Sabellianis, qui
vocantur etiam Patripassiani, catholica fides damnat: sed
quod tam similes sint Pater et Filius, ut qui unum noverit,
ambos noverit. Solemus enim de simillimis duobus ita loqui
eis qui unum illorum vident et qualis est alius volunt nosse,
ut dicamus, Vidistis istum, illum vidistis. Sic ergo dictum
est: *Qui me videt, videt et Patrem:* non utique ut ipse sit
Pater qui Filius, sed quod a Patris similitudine in nullo
prorsus discrepet Filius. Nam nisi duo essent Pater et Filius,
non dictum esset, *Si cognovistis me, et Patrem meum cognovistis.* Utique enim, quia *nemo*, inquit, *venit ad Patrem nisi
per me ; si cognovistis me, et Patrem meum cognovistis:* quoniam ego per quem venitur ad Patrem, perducam vos ad eum,
ut ipsum etiam cognoscatis. Sed quoniam illi sum omnino
simillimus, *amodo cognoscetis eum,* cum cognoscetis me: *et
vidistis eum,* si *oculis cordis* (Eph. i. 18) vidistis me.

3. Quid ergo est quod dicis, Philippe : *Ostende nobis
Patrem, et sufficit nobis ?* *Tanto*, inquit, *tempore vobiscum
sum, et non cognovistis me, Philippe ?* *Qui videt me, videt et
Patrem.* Quod si ad te multum est hoc videre, saltem quod
non vides hoc crede. *Quomodo* enim *dicis*, inquit, *ostende
nobis Patrem ?* Si me vidisti qui omnimodo similis sum,
vidisti illum cui similis sum. Quod si videre non potes,

am one Person, He is another. But that they may not think Him unlike, He adds, *And from henceforth ye shall know Him, and have seen Him.* They saw one very like to Him, His Son, but had to be instructed that the Father, whom they saw not yet, is even such as is the Son whom they beheld. And this is the import of those later words to Philip, *He that seeth Me, seeth the Father also.* Not that He was both Father and Son, which thing the Catholic faith condemns in the Sabellians or Patripassians as they are also called ; but because Father and Son are so alike that he who knows the one knows both. When two men are very much alike, in speaking of them to those who see the one and wish to know what kind the other is, we are wont to say, If you have seen the one, you have seen the other. In this sense then it is said, *He that seeth Me, seeth the Father also,* not of course that He who is Son is likewise Father, but because the Son is in all respects the perfect likeness of the Father. For unless the Father and the Son were two, it would not have been said, *If ye have known Me, ye have known My Father also.* For He says, you know, that *no man cometh unto the Father but by Me ; if ye have known Me, ye have known My Father also ;* since I, by whom men come to the Father, will lead you to Him, that ye may know Him also. But because I am altogether like to Him, *from henceforth ye shall know Him,* as soon as ye shall know Me ; *and ye have seen Him,* if *with the eyes of your heart* (Eph. i. 18) ye have seen Me.

3. What is this then that thou sayest, O Philip, *Shew us the Father, and it sufficeth us* ? *Have I,* saith the Lord, *been so long time with you, and have ye not known Me, Philip ? He that seeth Me, seeth the Father also.* But if it is too hard a thing for thee to see this much, at least believe this which thou seest not. For *how sayest thou,* saith Christ, *shew us the Father ?* If thou hast seen Me, who am His perfect likeness in every way, thou hast seen Him whom I am like. But if thou canst not see, *dost thou not* at least *believe that I am in*

non saltem *credis quia ego in Patre, et Pater in me est?*
Poterat hic dicere Philippus: Video quidem te, et credo
simillimum esse Patri; sed numquid arguendus et objurgandus
est, qui cum similem videt, etiam illum cui similis est vult
videre? Similem quidem novi, sed adhuc alterum sine altero
novi; non mihi sufficit, nisi et illum cuius est iste similis
noverim. *Ostende* itaque *nobis Patrem, et sufficit nobis.* Sed
ideo magister discipulum arguebat, quoniam cor postulantis
videbat. Tamquam enim melior esset Pater quam Filius, ita
Philippus Patrem nosse cupiebat: et ideo nec Filium sciebat,
quo melius esse aliquid credebat. Ad hunc sensum corrigendum
dictum est, *Qui videt me, videt et Patrem. Quomodo tu dicis,
Ostende nobis Patrem?* Video quomodo tu dicas: non alterum
quaeris videre similem, sed illum putas esse meliorem. *Non
credis quia ego in Patre, et Pater in me est?* Cur in similibus
distantiam cupis cernere? cur inseparabiles separatim desideras
nosse? Deinde non ad solum Philippum, sed ad eos pluraliter
loquitur, quae non sunt in angustias coarctanda, ut adiuvante
ipso diligentius exponantur.

TRACTATUS LXXI.

In id quod Dominus dicit: *Verba quae ego loquor vobis, a me
ipso non loquor,* usque ad id: *Si quid petieritis Patrem in
nomine meo, hoc faciam* (xiv. 10—14).

1. Audite auribus, accipite mentibus, dilectissimi, loquen-
tibus quidem nobis, sed ipso docente qui non recedit a nobis.
Dominus dicit, quod modo cum legeretur audistis: *Verba*

the Father, and the Father in Me? Here Philip might answer, I do indeed see Thee, and believe Thee to be altogether like the Father; but is he to be reproved and blamed, who, when he sees one like another, wishes to see the other whom he is like? I know the likeness, but as yet I do but know the one without the other: I am not satisfied unless I also know him whom he is like. *Shew us* then *the Father, and it sufficeth us.* But the reason why the Master rebuked the enquiry of the disciple was because He read his heart. For Philip asked to know the Father, as though the Father were better than the Son; and hence he did not even know the Son, because he deemed there could be aught better than He. To correct this thought Christ said, *He that seeth Me, seeth the Father also. How sayest thou, Shew us the Father?* I see the motive of thy demand; thou dost not seek to see the other who is like to Me, thou thinkest that He is better than I. *Believest thou not that I am in the Father, and the Father in Me?* Why wouldest thou discover a difference in them that are alike? Why desirest thou to know apart those that may not be parted? His next utterance, which is addressed not now to Philip by himself but to the disciples in the plural, does not allow of summary compression, but requires to be set forth with His help, and all the care we can bestow.

HOMILY LXXI.

On the Lord's words : *The words that I speak unto you, I speak not of Myself,* as far as : *If ye shall ask the Father anything in My name, I will do it* (xiv. 10—14).

1. Lend your ears, open your minds, my dearly beloved, for, although I am the speaker, the teacher is the Lord who leaves us not. He says, what ye heard read just now, *The*

quae ego loquor vobis, a me ipso non loquor : Pater autem in me manens ipse facit opera. Ergo et verba opera sunt ? Plane ita est. Nam profecto qui proximum loquendo aedificat, bonum opus operatur. Sed quid est, *a me ipso non loquor*, nisi a me ipso non sum qui loquor ? Ei quippe tribuit quod facit, de quo est ipse qui facit. Pater enim Deus non est de aliquo, Filius autem Deus est quidem Patri aequalis, sed de Patre Deo. Ideo ille Deus, sed non de Deo ; et lumen, sed non de lumine : iste vero Deus de Deo, lumen de lumine.

2. Nam in his duabus sententiis, una qua dictum est, *Non a me ipso loquor ;* alia qua dictum est, *Pater autem in me manens ipse facit opera*, singulas tenentes, diversi nobis adversantur haeretici, qui non ex una parte, sed in contraria conantes, a via veritatis exorbitant. Ariani quippe dicunt : Ecce inaequalis est Patri Filius, a se ipso non loquitur. Dicunt Sabelliani contra, id est, Patripassiani : Ecce qui Pater est ipse et Filius ; quid enim est, *Pater in me manens ipse facit opera*, nisi in me maneo ego qui facio ? Contraria dicitis : sed non eo modo sicut est falsum contrarium vero, sed sicut sunt inter se duo falsa contraria. Errando in diversa istis, in medio est via quam reliquistis. Inter vos ipsos longiore intervallo separati estis, quam ab ipsa via, cuius desertores estis. Vos hinc, vos autem illinc, huc venite : alteri ad alteros transire nolite, sed hinc atque illinc ad nos veniendo, invicem vos invenite. Sabelliani, agnoscite quem praetermittitis ; Ariani, aequate quem subditis, et in via vera nobiscum ambulabitis. Est enim quod invicem ex vobis alteri ex alteris admoneri utrique debeatis. Audi, Sabelliane : usque

words that I speak unto you, I speak not of Myself: but the Father that dwelleth in Me, He doeth the works. Are words then likewise works? Clearly they are. For undoubtedly he that by speech edifies his neighbour works a good work. But what meaneth, *I speak not of Myself,* unless, "I that speak am not of Myself"? He attributes what He does to Him from whom He Himself, the doer, is. For God the Father is from no one; while God the Son is indeed equal with the Father, but from God the Father. Therefore the Father is God, but not from God; light, but not from light: but the Son is God from God, light from light.

2. These two sentences, the one which says, *I speak not of Myself,* and the other which says, *But the Father that dwelleth in Me, He doeth the works,* are severally held and advanced against us by two different sects of heretics, not working together but in opposition to each other, and both wandering wide of the way of truth. The Arians say, Behold, the Son is not equal to the Father; He speaketh not of Himself. The Sabellians, or Patripassians, on the other hand, declare, He who is Father is also Son; for what is meant, they ask, by *The Father that dwelleth in Me, He doeth the works,* but, I that do them dwell in Myself? These are contrary assertions; not contrary in the way in which false is contrary to true, but as two false things are contrary to each other. Ye have lost your way in different directions; the way ye have abandoned lies between you. Ye are further apart from each other than from the very way ye have forsaken. Come you hither, you from this side, and you from that; cross not over to the other's side, but come from this side and from that, and find each other here with us. Sabellians, acknowledge Him ye disregard; Arians, give Him whom ye subordinate His equal rank, and you will both be walking with us in the way of truth. There is a lesson which each of you in turn is bound to learn from the other. Hear, O Sabellian: so certain is it that the Son is not the Father

adeo non ipse Pater, sed alter est Filius, ut eum Arianus inaequalem asserat Patri. Audi, Ariane : usque adeo Filius aequalis est Patri, ut Sabellianus eundem esse dicat et Patrem. Tu adde quem tollis, tu adimple quem minuis, et nobiscum ambo consistitis : quia nec tu tollis, nec tu minuis eum qui et alter est a Patre, ut convincas Sabellianum, et aequalis Patri, ut convincas Arianum. Utrisque enim clamat : *Ego et Pater unum sumus* (Ioan. x. 30). Quod ait, *unum*, audiant Ariani ; quod ait, *sumus*, audiant Sabelliani : et nec illi aequalem, nec illi alterum negando sint vani. Si ergo quoniam dixit : *Verba quae ego loquor vobis, a me ipso non loquor*, propterea putatur usque adeo imparis potestatis, ut non quod ipse vult faciat : audiatur quod dixit : *Sicut Pater suscitat mortuos et vivificat, sic et Filius quos vult vivificat* (ib. v. 21). Item si quoniam dixit : *Pater in me manens ipse facit opera*, propterea putatur non alius esse Pater, alius ipse ; audiatur quod dixit : *Quae-cunque Pater facit, haec et Filius similiter facit* (ib. v. 19) : et intelligatur non bis unus, sed duo unum. Verum quia sic aequalis alter alteri, ut tamen alter ex altero, ideo non loquitur a semetipso, quia non est a se ipso : et ideo *Pater in illo manens facit opera ipse*, quia per quem et cum quo facit, non est nisi ab ipso. Denique adiungit et dicit : *Non creditis quia ego in Patre, et Pater in me est ? Alioquin propter opera ipsa credite* (ib. xiv. 11). Antea solus Philippus arguebatur, nunc autem non ibi eum solum fuisse qui esset arguendus

but another, that the Arian maintains Him to be inferior
to the Father; and hear, O Arian: so surely is the Son
the Father's equal that the Sabellian declares Him to be
identical with the Father. Add, thou, Him whom thou
omittest; and complete, thou, Him whom thou impairest;
so shall ye both stand side by side with us. For you, Arian,
as things are, do not disregard, nor do you, Sabellian, impair,
Him who is not only different from the Father (a proof against
the Sabellian), but also equal to the Father (a proof against
the Arian). To both of you He cries: *I and the Father are
one* (Jn. x. 30). When He says *one*, let the Arian, when He
says *are*, let the Sabellian hearken; and let both alike cease
from their folly in denying, the one, that He is equal, the
other, that He is different. If then because He said:
The words which I speak unto you, I speak not of Myself,
He is therefore accounted of such inferior power that He
doeth not what He Himself wills, hear ye His words: *As
the Father raiseth the dead and quickeneth them, so also
the Son quickeneth whom He wills* (ib. v. 21). Again, if because He said, *The Father that dwelleth in Me, He doeth
the works*, it is therefore thought that the Father is not
one and He another, hear His words, *What things soever the
Father doeth, these also the Son in like manner doeth* (ib.
v. 19), and let it be understood that here we have not
one person twice repeated, but two persons joined in one.
But because the one is equal to the other and yet the
one is from the other, for this cause He speaketh not of
Himself, because He is not of Himself; and therefore *the
Father that dwelleth in* Him, *He doeth the works*, because He
by whom and with whom the Father does them, derives His
existence from Him. Finally He goes on to say, *Believe
ye not that I am in the Father, and the Father in Me? at
least believe Me for the very works' sake* (ib. xiv. 11).
Philip only was reproved before; but now it is made clear
that he was not the only one there to need reproof. *For the*

ostenditur. *Propter opera*, inquit, *ipsa credite, quia ego in Patre et Pater in me est:* neque enim si separati essemus, inseparabiliter operari ulla ratione possemus.

3. Sed quid est quod sequitur : *Amen, amen dico vobis, qui credit in me, opera quae ego facio, et ipse faciet, et maiora horum faciet, quia ego ad Patrem vado ; et quaecunque petieritis in nomine meo, haec faciam, ut glorificetur Pater in Filio: si quid petieritis in nomine meo, hoc faciam* ? Ergo et illa maiora opera se ipsum facturum esse promisit. Non se extollat servus supra Dominum, et discipulus supra Magistrum : maiora quam ipse facit dicit eos esse facturos ; sed in eis vel per eos se faciente, non ipsis tamquam ex se ipsis. Ei quippe cantatur : *Diligam te, Domine, virtus mea* (Psal. xvii. 2). Sed quae sunt tandem ista maiora ? An forte quod aegros, ipsis transeuntibus, etiam eorum umbra sanabat (Act. v. 15) ? Maius est enim ut sanet umbra quam fimbria. Illud per se, hoc per ipsos, sed tamen utrumque ipse. Verumtamen quando ista dicebat, verborum suorum opera commendabat : sic enim dixerat : *Verba quae ego loquor vobis, a me ipso non loquor, Pater autem in me manens ipse facit opera.* Quae opera tunc dicebat, nisi verba quae loquebatur ? Audiebant et credebant illi, et eorundem verborum fructus erat fides illorum : verumtamen evangelizantibus discipulis, non tam pauci quam illi erant, sed gentes etiam crediderunt, haec sunt sine dubitatione maiora. Nec tamen ait : Maiora horum facietis, ut solos apostolos ea putaremus esse facturos : sed, *Qui credit in me*, inquit, *opera quae ego facio, et ipse faciet, et maiora horum faciet.* Itane quicunque credit in Christum,

very works' sake, He saith, *believe ye that I am in the Father and the Father in Me;* for were we separated, by no means could we work inseparably.

3. But what is this which follows, *Verily, verily, I say unto you, He that believeth in Me, the works that I do shall he do also; and greater works than these shall he do, because I go unto the Father; and what things soever ye shall ask in My name, these will I do, that the Father may be glorified in the Son: if ye shall ask anything in My name, I will do it*? Thus even those greater works He promised He would do Himself. Let not the servant uplift himself above his Lord, nor the disciple above his Master; He says that they shall do greater works than He doeth, but it is He that doeth them in them or else by them, not they themselves as of themselves. To Him we sing, *I will love thee, O Lord, my strength* (Ps. xviii. 1). Now what are these greater works? Was it that, as they passed by, their very shadow healed the sick (Acts v. 15)? It is a greater work for a shadow than for the hem of a garment to have power to heal. He wrought the one work by Himself, the other by their means; yet He wrought both. When however He spake these words, it was the works of His words to which He called attention, for He had said on this wise, *The words which I speak unto you, I speak not of Myself: but the Father that dwelleth in Me, He doeth the works.* What works did He mean then, but the words which He was speaking? The disciples heard and believed, and the fruit of those words was their faith; but when they preached the Gospel, it was no longer a small company, such as they were, that believed, but whole nations: here are without doubt greater works. And He does not say, "Greater than these shall ye do," in such a way that we should think that the Apostles alone would do them, but, *He that believeth in Me, the works that I do shall he do, and greater works than these shall he do.* Doth he then, whosoever believeth on Christ, do what Christ

facit quae Christus, vel maiora quam Christus? Non praetereunter ista tractanda sunt, nec debent festinatione prae-
cipitari ; sed ea cogit concludendus iam sermo iste differri.

TRACTATUS LXXII.

In eandem lectionem (xiv. 12).

1. Quid sibi velit et quomodo accipiendum sit quod
Dominus ait : *Qui credit in me, opera quae ego facio et ipse
faciet,* non est facile comprehendere : et cum hoc ad intelligendum difficillimum sit, adiecit aliud difficilius : *Et maiora
horum faciet.* Quid est hoc ? Qui faceret opera quae Christus
fecit, non inveniebamus ; qui etiam maiora faciet, inventuri
sumus ? Sed dixeramus sermone pristino quia maius fuit
umbrae suae transitu, quod discipuli fecerunt, quam fimbriae
suae tactu, quod ipse Dominus fecit, sanare languentes ; et
quia plures apostolis, quam ipso per os proprium praedicante
Domino crediderunt : ut haec viderentur opera intelligenda
esse maiora : non quo maior esset Magistro discipulus, vel
Domino servus, vel adoptatus Unigenito, vel homo Deo ; sed
quod per illos ipse dignaretur eadem maiora facere, qui dicit
illis alio loco : *Sine me nihil potestis facere* (Ioan. xv. 5).
Ipse quippe, ut alia omittam quae sunt innumerabilia, sine
ipsis fecit eos, sine ipsis fecit hunc mundum ; et quia homo
etiam ipse fieri dignatus est, sine ipsis fecit et se ipsum.
Quid autem illi sine ipso nisi peccatum ? Denique et hic id,
quod de hac re poterat nos movere, mox abstulit : cum enim
dixisset : *Qui credit in me, opera quae ego facio et ipse faciet,*

doeth, or even greater works than Christ? Here is matter
that may not be cursorily handled nor quickly hurried over ;
but it must be deferred, for it is time to close my sermon.

HOMILY LXXII.

On the same lection (xiv. 12).

1.   It is not easy to grasp the meaning and proper accep-
tation of the Lord's words : *He that believeth in Me, the
works that I do shall he do also;* and difficult as this
utterance is to understand, He has added another yet more
difficult : *and greater than these shall he do.* What is this ?
We could not find a man to do the works that Christ did ;
are we likely to find one who shall do even greater ? Now we
said in the last sermon that it was a greater work to heal
the sick by the casting of one's shadow, as the disciples did,
than by contact with the border of one's mantle, as the Lord
did ; and that more believed on the apostles than believed
when our Lord was preaching with His own lips ; so that
these clearly were the works which we must understand to be
the greater works : not that the disciple was to be greater than
his Master, or the servant than his Lord, or the adopted than
the Only-Begotten Sͻn, or man than God ; but because it was
by these agents that He deigned to work these greater works,
He who saith to them elsewhere : *Without Me ye can do
nothing* (Jn. xv. 5).   On the other hand—to say nothing of
His other countless acts—without them He made them, without them He made this world of ours ; yea without them, in
that He condescended to be made man, He made Himself.
But what without Him did they produce but sin ? Accordingly
all our difficulty on this point is quickly removed by this
same passage ; for after saying : *He that believeth in Me, the*

et maiora horum faciet; continuo secutus adiunxit : *Quia ego
ad Patrem vado, et quaecunque petieritis in nomine meo, haec
faciam.* Qui dixerat *faciet*, post ait *faciam*, tamquam diceret,
Non vobis impossibile hoc videatur : non enim poterit esse maior
me qui credit in me, sed ego facturus sum et tunc maiora quam
nunc ; maiora per eum qui credit in me, quam praeter eum per
me : ego tamen ipse praeter eum, ego ipse per eum : sed quando
praeter eum, non faciet ipse ; quando autem per eum, quamvis
non per semetipsum, faciet et ipse. Porro autem maiora
facere per eum quam praeter eum, non est defectio, sed
dignatio. Quid enim retribuant servi *Domino pro omnibus
quae retribuit* eis (Psal. cxv. .12) ? Quandoquidem inter
cetera bona etiam hoc eis donare dignatus est, ut maiora
faceret per illos quam praeter illos. Nonne ab ore illius dives
ille tristis abscessit, quando vitae aeternae consilium quaesivit (Matth. xix. 22) ? Audivit, abiecit : et tamen postea
quod ab illo auditum non fecit unus, fecerunt multi, cum
loqueretur per discipulos Magister bonus ; contemptibilis ei
quem divitem per se ipsum monuit, amabilis eis quos ex
divitibus pauperes per pauperes fecit. Ecce maiora fecit
praedicatus a credentibus, quam locutus audientibus.

2. Verum hoc adhuc movet, quod haec maiora per
apostolos fecit : non autem ipsos tantum significans ait :
Opera quae ego facio et vos facietis, et maiora horum facietis :
sed omnes ad suam familiam pertinentes intelligi volens, *qui
credit in me,* inquit, *opera quae ego facio, et ipse faciet, et*

*works which I do shall he do also, and greater works than
these shall he do*, He straightway went on to add: *Because
I go to the Father, and what things soever ye shall ask in My
name, these will I do.* He who had said, *he shall do*, saith
afterwards, *I will do;* as much as to say, Let not this seem
to you impossible; he who believeth in Me cannot indeed
be greater than I, but I hereafter will do greater works than
now; greater, through him that believeth in Me, than by
Myself apart from him; whether apart from him or through
him, it is still I Myself that do them; but when they are done
apart from him, it will not be he that doeth; when they are
done through him, it will be he that doeth, albeit not by
himself. Moreover to do through man works greater than
apart from man, argues not weakness but condescension. For
what can servants render *unto the Lord for all that He hath
rendered* unto them (Ps. cxvi. 12), seeing that with all their
other blessings he hath deigned to bestow upon them the
further privilege, that the works He wrought through them
should be greater than those He wrought apart from them?
Did not the rich man in the Gospel go sadly from His presence,
when he sought counsel concerning eternal life (Mt. xix. 22)?
He heard and he rejected; and yet what one refused to do, when
bidden by the Master, was presently done by many, when
the good Master spake by His disciples. Slighted by the
rich man whom He warned with His own lips, He was
beloved by those whom, being rich, He rendered poor through
poor men's preaching. Yea Christ, when He was preached
by those who believed in Him, did greater works than when
He spake Himself to men who would listen.

2. But there is still this difficulty; these *greater works*
He did by His Apostles, whereas He does not mean them
only when He says: *the works which I do shall ye do also,
and greater works than these shall ye do;* but because He
wished it to be understood of all belonging to His household,
He saith: *He that believeth in Me, the works which I do*

maiora horum faciet. Si ergo qui credit faciet, non credit
utique qui non faciet; sicuti est, *Qui diligit me, mandata mea
custodit* (Ioan. xiv. 21) : unde profecto qui non custodit, non
diligit. Item alio loco : *Qui audit,* inquit, *verba mea haec, et
facit ea, similabo eum viro prudenti, qui aedificat domum
suam supra petram* (Matth. vii. 24) : qui ergo non est similis
huic viro prudenti, procul dubio aut verba haec audit et non
facit, aut omnino nec audit. *Qui credit,* inquit, *in me, licet
moriatur, vivet* (Ioan. xi. 25) ; qui ergo non vivet, non utique
credit. Tale etiam hoc est : *Qui credit in me, faciet :* non
utique, credit qui non faciet. Quid est hoc, fratres ? Numquid inter credentes in Christum non est computandus, qui
non fecerit opera maiora quam Christus ? Durum est, absur-
dum est, ferri non potest : non toleratur nisi intelligatur.
Apostolum igitur audiamus : *Credenti,* inquit, *in eum qui
iustificat impium, deputatur fides ejus ad iustitiam* (Rom. iv.
5). In hoc opere faciamus opera Christi, quia et ipsum
credere in Christum, opus est Christi. Hoc operatur in
nobis, non utique sine nobis. Audi ergo iam et intellige :
Qui credit in me, opera quae ego facio et ipse faciet : prius
ego facio, deinde et ipse faciet ; quia facio ut faciat. Quae
opera, nisi ut ex impio iustus fiat ?

3. *Et maiora horum faciet.* Quorum ? obsecro. Numquidnam omnium operum Christi maiora facit, qui *cum
timore et tremore* suam ipsius *salutem operatur* (Philip. ii. 12) ?
Quod utique in illo, sed non sine illo Christus operatur.
Prorsus maius hoc esse dixerim, quam est caelum et terra, et
quaecunque cernuntur in caelo et in terra. Et *caelum* enim *et
terra transibit* (Matth. xxiv. 35) : praedestinatorum autem,
id est, eorum quos praescit, salus et iustificatio permanebit.

shall he do also, and greater works than these shall he do. If
then he who believes shall do, he that shall not do is no
believer; just as, *He that loveth Me, keepeth My commandments* (Jn. xiv. 21), implies that he loveth not who doth
not keep. Again, in another place He says: *He that heareth
these words of Mine and doeth them, I will liken him unto a
wise man that buildeth his house upon a rock* (Mt. vii. 24); he
therefore that is not like this wise man, does doubtless either
hear these words and doeth them not, or else he fails to hear
them altogether. *He that believeth in Me,* He says, *though he die,
yet shall he live* (Jn. xi. 25); hence surely he that shall not live,
does not believe. This saying also is just the same: *He that
believeth in Me, shall do;* not of course, he believes that shall
not do. What is this, my brethren? Are we then not to
reckon among Christ's believers a man who does not do
greater works than Christ? This is hard, absurd, intolerable;
intolerable it is, if it be not understood. Hear therefore the
Apostle: *To him that believeth on Him that justifieth the ungodly, his faith is counted unto him for righteousness* (Rom.
iv. 5). In this work let us do the works of Christ, for the
mere believing in Christ is Christ's own work; for this He
works in us, though not apart from us. Hear then and
understand, *He that believeth in Me, the works that I do shall
he do also.* First I work them, then too he shall work
them; I work them that he may work them. Work what
but the conversion of a man from sin to righteousness?

3. *And greater than these shall he do.* Greater than
what? I ask. Is that man doing greater than all Christ's
works who *with fear and trembling worketh out his own
salvation* (Phil. ii. 12)? a work which certainly is wrought in
him by Christ, though not apart from him. Yes, this in
truth I would dare call a really greater work than heaven
and earth, than anything we see in earth and heaven. For
both *heaven and earth shall pass away* (Mt. xxiv. 35) but the
salvation and justification of the predestinated, i.e. of those

In illis tantum opera Dei, in his autem etiam est imago Dei.
Sed et *in caelis sedes, dominationes, principatus, potestates*
(Col. i. 16), archangeli, angeli, opera sunt Christi : numquid
etiam his operibus maiora facit qui, operante in se Christo,
cooperatur aeternam salutem ac iustificationem suam ?   Non
hic audeo praecipitare sententiam : intelligat qui potest, iudicet
qui potest, utrum maius sit iustos creare quam impios
iustificare.   Certe enim si aequalis est utrumque potentiae,
hoc maioris est misericordiae.   Hoc est enim *magnum pietatis*
sacramentum, quod manifestatum est in carne, iustificatum est
in spiritu, apparuit angelis, praedicatum est in gentibus,
creditum est in mundo, assumptum est in gloria (1 Tim. iii.
16).   Sed omnia opera Christi intelligere ubi ait, *Maiora horum*
faciet, nulla nos necessitas cogit.   Horum enim forsitan dixit,
quae in illa hora faciebat : tunc autem verba fidei faciebat, et
de his operibus fuerat praelocutus dicens : *Verba quae ego*
loquor vobis, a me ipso non loquor, Pater autem in me manens
ipse facit opera (Ioan. xiv. 10).   Tunc igitur verba eius erant
opera eius.   Et utique minus est verba iustitiae praedicare,
quod fecit praeter nos, quam impios iustificare, quod ita facit
in nobis, ut faciamus et nos.   Restat inquirere quomodo
accipiendum sit, *Quodcunque petieritis in nomine meo, hoc*
faciam.   Propter multa enim quae petunt fideles ejus, nec
accipiunt, non parva hinc exoritur quaestio : sed quoniam
sermo iste iam claudendus est, ei considerandae atque trac-
tandae tribuatur saltem parva dilatio.

whom He foreknoweth, shall abide for ever. For in those things we see only the works of God, but in these men His very image as well. Yet *the thrones, dominions, principalities, powers,* archangels and angels, which also are *in heaven* (Col. i. 16), are the works of Christ; doth he work greater works than these who, with Christ working in him, helps to work out his own eternal salvation and justification? I dare not here give hasty sentence; let him understand who can, judge who can, which work is greater, to create the righteous, or to justify the ungodly. At least if both are works of equal power, the latter hath more of mercy. For this is *the great mystery of godliness, which was manifested in the flesh, was justified in the spirit, appeared unto angels, was preached among the Gentiles, was believed in the world, was taken up in glory* (1 Tim. iii. 16). But there is no need to understand all the works of Christ when He says : *greater than these shall he do.* By *these* perchance He meant the works He was doing in that hour ; now His work at that hour was His preaching of the faith, and of this He had earlier spoken, when He said : *The words which I speak to you, I speak not of Myself : but the Father that dwelleth in Me, He doeth the works* (Jn. xiv. 10). At that hour therefore His words were His works. And surely it is something less to preach the words of righteousness, which He did apart from us, than to justify the ungodly, which He does now in us, yet in such a way that it is also our doing. The question now remains how we are to take, *Whatsoever ye shall ask in My name, I will do it.* No small difficulty arises from the fact that His believers ask many things which they do not receive; but since this sermon must now end, we must put off at least for a little the consideration and treatment of the subject.

TRACTATUS LXXIII.

Item in eandem lectionem (xiv. 12—14).

1.   Magnam spem Dominus suis promisit sperantibus,
dicens : *Quia ego ad Patrem vado, et quodcunque petieritis in
nomine meo, hoc faciam.*   Sic ergo perrexit ad Patrem, ut non
relinqueret indigentes, sed exaudiret petentes.   Sed quid est,
quodcunque petieritis, cum videamus plerumque fideles ejus
petere, et non accipere ?   An forte propterea quia male
petunt ?   Nam hoc exprobravit apostolus Iacobus dicens :
*Petitis, et non accipitis, eo quod male petatis, ut in concupis-
centiis vestris insumatis* (Iacob. iv. 3).   Male ergo usurus eo
quod vult accipere, Deo potius miserante non accipit.   Proinde
si hoc ab illo petitur, unde homo laedatur exauditus, magis
metuendum est, ne quod posset non dare propitius, det iratus.
Annon videmus Israelitas malo suo impetrasse, quod culpabili
concupiscentia petierunt (Num. xi. 32) ?   Concupierant enim
carnibus vesci, quibus pluebatur manna de caelo.   Fastidiebant
quippe quod habebant, et quod non habebant, impudenter
petebant : quasi non melius peterent, non ut cibus qui deerat
indecenti desiderio praestaretur, sed ut ille qui aderat sanato
fastidio sumeretur.   Quando enim nos delectant mala et non
delectant bona, rogare debemus potius Deum, ut delectent
bona, quam ut concedantur mala.   Non quia malum est carne
vesci, cum de hac re loquens Apostolus dicat : *Omnis creatura
Dei bona est, et nihil abiciendum quod cum gratiarum actione
accipitur* (1 Tim. iv. 4) : sed quia sicut item ipse ait : *Malum
est homini qui per offensionem manducat* (Rom. xiv. 20) ; et si

HOMILY LXXIII.

Also on the same lection (xiv. 12—14).

1. The promise of a glorious hope was given by the Lord to those whose hope is in Him, when He said : *Because I go to the Father, and whatsoever ye shall ask in My name, I will do it.* Thus He went to the Father, in such a manner that He did not leave them in want, but heard their petitions. But what is the meaning of, *Whatsoever ye shall ask*, when we so often find His believers asking and not receiving ? Is it because they ask amiss ? The Apostle James made this thing matter of accusation, saying, *Ye ask, and receive not, because ye ask amiss, that ye may spend it upon your lusts* (Jas. iv. 3). When therefore a man is going to use amiss that which he would receive, it is rather God's mercy that he receives it not. Thus if a man seeks aught from God which would harm him if his prayer were granted, we should rather fear lest what God could not give in mercy, He may give in anger. Do we not see that the Israelites obtained that to their hurt which they sought in guilty lust (Num. xi. 32) ? They had lusted to have flesh to eat, while manna rained on them from heaven. Loathing what they had, they felt no shame in asking for what they had not ; as though they would not have done better to ask that they might be cured of their loathing and take the food before them, rather than that food which they had not might be given them to glut disgraceful greed. For when we find pleasure in what is ill, and none in what is good, we ought to pray God rather to give us power to enjoy the good than to grant the ill. Not that it is wrong to eat flesh, for the Apostle speaking on this very point says : *Every creature of God is good, and nothing is to be rejected that is received with thanksgiving* (1 Tim. iv. 4), but because as he himself says elsewhere, *It is evil for that man who eateth with offence* (Rom. xiv. 20) ; and if it is evil when it offends man,

hominis offensionem, quanto magis Dei? Cujus in Israëlitis
non parva erat offensio, repudiare quod dabat sapientia,
et petere id quod inhiabat concupiscentia; quamvis illi nec
peterent, sed quia deerat murmurarent. Sed ut sciremus non
Dei creaturam esse culpabilem, sed inobedientiam contumacem
et inordinatam cupiditatem: non propter porcum, sed propter
pomum mortem primus homo invenit, et Esau primatus suos
non propter gallinam, sed propter lenticulam perdidit (Gen.
xxv. 34).

2. Quomodo ergo intelligendum est: *Quodcunque petie-*
ritis, hoc faciam, si Deus aliqua petentibus fidelibus etiam
consulendo non facit? An forte solis apostolis dictum
debemus accipere? absit. Unde enim ad hoc venit ut diceret,
superius dixerat: *Qui credit in me, opera quae ego facio faciet,*
et maiora horum faciet: de qua re pristino sermone tracta-
vimus. Et ne quisquam hoc sibi retribueret, ut etiam illa
opera maiora se ipsum facere ostenderet, adiecit atque ait:
Quia ego ad Patrem vado, et quodcunque petieritis in nomine
meo, hoc faciam. Numquid in eum soli apostoli crediderunt?
Ad eos itaque loquebatur dicendo, *qui credit in me,* in quibus
eo donante etiam nos sumus, qui utique non quodcunque
petierimus accipimus. Ipsos quoque beatissimos si cogitemus
apostolos, invenimus eum qui *plus omnibus laboravit, non*
autem ipse, sed gratia Dei cum ipso, ter Dominum rogasse ut
ab eo discederet angelus satanae (1 Cor. xv. 10; 2 Cor. xii.
7, 8), nec tamen quod rogaverat accepisse. Quid dicimus,
carissimi? Putabimusne hoc promissum ubi ait: *Quod-*
cunque petieritis hoc faciam, nec apostolis fuisse ab illo
completum? Et cui tandem quod promittit implebit, si
apostolos suos in sua promissione fraudavit?

how much more evil when it offends God! And He had no
small cause of offence in the Israelites when they refused that
which Wisdom offered, and sought that for which lust craved;
though after all they did not seek it, but only murmured at
its absence. However that we might know that God's creature
is not to blame, but insolent disobedience and unbridled lust,
it was not swine's flesh but an apple that brought death upon
the first man, and Esau lost his birthright not for a pullet but
for pulse (Gen. xxv. 34).

2. How then are we to understand: *Whatsoever ye shall
ask, I will do it,* if there are some things which the faithful
ask and which God of set purpose does not do? Ought we to
take the utterance as spoken only to the Apostles? God
forbid! The Lord had previously said: *He that believeth in
Me, the works that I do shall he do also, and greater works
than these shall he do;* that was the starting-point from which
He reached the utterance in question, and we dealt with it in
a previous discourse. Now that none might take the merit
to himself, and in order to shew that even those *greater works*
were done by Him, He further added: *Because I go to the
Father, and whatsoever ye shall ask in My name, I will do it.*
Is it only the Apostles, I ask, that have believed in Him?
Nay, when He said, *He that believeth in Me,* He spake to
those among whom we also by His grace are numbered, and
we certainly do not receive whatsoever we ask. And indeed
if we recall to mind the blessed Apostles themselves, we find
that he who *laboured more than they all, yet not he, but the
grace of God which was with him, besought the Lord thrice,
that the messenger of Satan might depart from him* (1 Cor. xv.
10; 2 Cor. xii. 7, 8), and yet did not receive that which he
had asked for. What shall we say, beloved? Are we to think
that He did not fulfil even to His Apostles the promise,
Whatsoever ye shall ask I will do it? To whom will He ever
fulfil His promise, if He cheated His own Apostles of the
promise made to them?

4—2

3. Evigila igitur, homo fidelis, et vigilanter audi quod illic positum est, *in nomine meo* : ipsum enim *quodcunque*, non ait, petieritis utcunque, sed *in nomine meo*. Qui promisit ergo tam magnum beneficium, quid vocatur ? Utique Christus Iesus : Christus significat regem, Iesus significat Salvatorem : non utique nos salvos faciet quicunque rex, sed rex Salvator : ac per hoc quodcunque petimus adversus utilitatem salutis, non petimus in nomine Salvatoris. Et tamen ipse Salvator est, non solum quando facit quod petimus, verum etiam quando non facit : quoniam quod videt peti contra salutem, non faciendo potius se exhibet Salvatorem. Novit enim medicus quid pro sua, quid contra suam salutem poscat aegrotus ; et ideo contraria poscentis non facit voluntatem, ut faciat sanitatem. Quapropter quando volumus ut faciat quodcunque petimus, non utcunque, sed in nomine eius petamus, hoc est in nomine Salvatoris petamus. Non ergo contra nostram salutem petamus : quod si fecerit, non ut Salvator facit, quod est nomen eius fidelibus eius. Est quippe impiis et damnator, qui dignatur fidelibus esse Salvator. Qui ergo credit in eum, quodcunque petierit in eo nomine, quod est illis qui credunt in eum, hoc facit : quoniam hoc sicut Salvator facit. Si autem qui in eum credit, aliquid per ignorantiam contra suam salutem petit, non in nomine Salvatoris petit : quia Salvator eius non erit, si quod eius salutem impedit fecerit. Unde tunc expedit potius, ut non faciendo propter quod invocatur faciat quod vocatur. Propterea non solum Salvator, sed etiam magister bonus, ut faciat quodcunque petierimus, in ipsa oratione quam nobis dedit, docuit quid petamus : ut etiam sic intelligamus non petere nos in nomine magistri, quod petimus praeter regulam ipsius magisterii.

3. Awake then, O man of faith, and lend a wakeful ear to the condition, *in My name*, herein laid down; for of the very "Whatsoever," He does not say, howsoever ye shall ask it, but *in My name*. By what name then is he called that hath promised this great blessing? Surely Christ Jesus; Christ means King, and Jesus, Saviour. And it is not any sort of king that shall save us, but a Saviour king; therefore whatsoever we ask that is against the interests of our salvation, we do not ask in the Saviour's name. And yet He is our Saviour, not only when He does what we ask, but also when He does it not; since when He sees us ask a thing contrary to our salvation, He shews Himself our real Saviour by not granting it. The physician knows whether what the patient asks is good or bad for his health, and when he asks what is bad, he refuses to do what he wishes, that he may make him well. Wherefore when we wish Him to do whatsoever we ask, let us ask it not anyhow, but in His name, i.e. let us ask in the Saviour's name. Let us not then ask for what is against our salvation; for if He does this, He does it not as Saviour, the name by which His faithful know Him. Ay, He who deigns to be Saviour to the faithful, is also doomsman to the ungodly. He does then whatsoever he that believes in Him shall ask in that name by which He is known to them who believe in Him, for He does it as Saviour. But if he that believes in Him asks through ignorance anything that is bad for his own salvation, he asks not in the Saviour's name; since He cannot be his Saviour, if He does aught to hinder his salvation. Hence in this case it is better that He should be true to His name by refusing the request. Accordingly since He is our good Master as well as our Saviour and would do whatsoever we ask, He hath in that prayer He gave us taught us what to ask; that in this way also we may learn that what we ask outside the rule of the Master's teaching we are not asking in the Master's name.

4. Sane quaedam, quamvis in nomine eius petamus, id
est secundum Salvatorem et secundum magistrum petamus;
non tunc quando petimus facit, sed tamen facit. Neque enim
quia et illud petimus ut *veniat regnum* Dei (Matth. vi. 10),
propterea non facit quod petimus, quia non statim cum illo
in aeternitate regnamus: differtur enim quod petimus, non
negatur. Verumtamen orantes tamquam seminantes *non de-*
ficiamus, tempore enim proprio metemus (Gal. vi. 9). Et simul
petamus quando bene petimus, ut non faciat quod non bene
petimus: quia et ad hoc pertinet quod in eadem oratione
dominica dicimus: *Ne nos inferas in tentationem* (Matth. vi. 13).
Neque enim parva est tentatio, si contra tuam sit causam tua
postulatio. Non autem negligenter audiendum est, quod
Dominus, ne quisquam eum putaret quod se promisit facere
petentibus, sine Patre esse facturum, cum dixisset, *Quodcun-*
que petieritis in nomine meo, hoc faciam, continuo subiecit:
Ut glorificetur Pater in Filio, si quid petieritis in nomine meo,
hoc faciam. Nullo modo igitur sine Patre hoc Filius facit,
quandoquidem ut in illo Pater glorificetur, propterea facit.
Facit ergo Pater in Filio, ut Filius glorificetur in Patre: et
facit Filius in Patre, ut Pater glorificetur in Filio; quoniam
unum sunt Pater et Filius.

TRACTATUS LXXIV.

De eo quod ait: *Si diligitis me, mandata mea servate,*
usque ad id: *Apud vos manebit, et in vobis erit* (xiv.
15—17).

1. Audivimus, fratres, cum Evangelium legeretur, Dominum dicentem: *Si diligitis me, mandata mea servate: et*

4. It is true that there are some things which, though we ask them in His name, i.e. remembering that He is both Saviour and Master, He does not at the time of our asking, but yet He does do them. Thus when we ask that the *kingdom* of God *may come* (Mt. vi. 10), we cannot say that He does not what we ask, because we do not straightway reign with Him in eternity for ever. What we ask is deferred, but not denied. Yet as in sowing, so in praying, *let us not faint; for in due season we shall reap* (Gal. vi. 9). And when we do ask aright, let us ask Him not to do what we ask not aright; for this too is included in the words we say in that same Lord's prayer, *Lead us not into temptation* (Mt. vi. 13). For the temptation is not trifling if thy request run counter to thy cause. Nor must we neglect to notice what the Lord added immediately after the words *Whatsoever ye shall ask in My name I will do it*, lest any should imagine that He would do apart from the Father what He promised to do to them that ask, viz. *That the Father may be glorified in the Son, if ye shall ask anything in My name, I will do it*. It is not then in any wise without the Father that the Son does this, since He does it that the Father may be glorified in Him. So the Father does it in the Son, that the Son may be glorified in the Father; and the Son does it in the Father, that the Father may be glorified in the Son, for Father and Son are One.

HOMILY LXXIV.

From the words: *If ye love me, keep my commandments*, as far as: *He shall dwell with you and shall be in you* (xiv. 15—17).

1. When the Gospel was read, my brethren, we heard the Lord say: *If ye love Me, keep my commandments; and I will*

ego rogabo Patrem, et alium Paracletum dabit vobis, ut maneat
vobiscum in aeternum, Spiritum veritatis, quem mundus non
potest accipere; quia non videt eum, nec scit eum. Vos autem
cognoscetis eum, quia apud vos manebit, et in vobis erit.
Multa sunt quae in istis paucis verbis Domini requirantur:
sed multum est ad nos vel omnia quae hic quaerenda sunt
quaerere, vel omnia quae hic quaerimus invenire. Verumtamen quantum nobis Dominus donare dignatur pro nostra
et vestra capacitate, quid dicere debeamus et quid audire
debeatis attendentes, per nos, carissimi, quod possumus
sumite, et ab illo quod non possumus poscite. Spiritum
Paracletum Christus promisit apostolis; quo autem modo
promiserit, advertamus. *Si diligitis me*, inquit, *mandata mea*
servate; et ego rogabo Patrem, et alium Paracletum dabit vobis,
ut maneat vobiscum in aeternum, Spiritum veritatis. Hic est
utique in Trinitate Spiritus sanctus, quem Patri et Filio
consubstantialem et coaeternum fides catholica confitetur: ipse
est de quo dicit Apostolus: *Caritas Dei diffusa est in cor-*
dibus nostris per Spiritum sanctum, qui datus est nobis (Rom.
v. 5). Quomodo ergo Dominus dicit: *Si diligitis me, mandata*
mea servate; et ego rogabo Patrem, et alium Paracletum dabit
vobis; cum hoc dicat de Spiritu sancto, quem nisi habeamus,
nec diligere Deum possumus, nec eius mandata servare? Quomodo diligimus ut eum accipiamus, quem nisi habeamus,
diligere non valemus? aut quomodo mandata servabimus, ut
eum accipiamus, quem nisi habeamus, mandata servare non
possumus? An forte praecedit in nobis caritas, qua diligimus Christum, ut diligendo Christum eiusque mandata
faciendo, mereamur accipere Spiritum sanctum, ut *caritas*
non Christi, quae iam praecesserat, sed *Dei* Patris *diffundatur*

pray the Father, and He shall give you another Paraclete, that He may abide with you for ever, even the Spirit of truth, whom the world cannot receive, because it seeth Him not, neither knoweth Him: but ye shall know Him, for He shall dwell with you, and shall be in you.

Much is there in this brief utterance of the Lord that courts enquiry; but it would be too hard a task for us to ask all the questions that can be asked, or find the answers to all the questions that we ask. Nevertheless, beloved, as far as the Lord is pleased to grant us, in proportion to our several capacities, what we ought to say and you to hear; pay heed and receive through us what we for our part are able to give, and ask of Him that wherein we fail.

Christ promised the Spirit as Paraclete to His Apostles; now let us note in what way He promised Him. *If ye love Me, keep My commandments; and I will pray the Father, and He shall give you another Paraclete, that He may abide with you for ever, even the Spirit of truth.* This is in very truth the Holy Spirit of the Trinity, whom the Catholic Faith confesses to be consubstantial and co-eternal with the Father and the Son; this is He of whom the Apostle says: *The love of God is shed abroad in our hearts by the Holy Spirit who was given unto us* (Rom. v. 5). How then doth the Lord say: *If ye love Me, keep My commandments; and I will pray the Father, and He shall give you another Paraclete,* seeing that He saith this of the Holy Spirit, whom if we have not, we can neither love God, nor keep His commandments? How are we to love, in order to receive Him, when, unless we have Him, we have no power to love? Or how shall we keep commandments, in order to receive Him, when, unless we have Him, we cannot keep commandments? Does perchance the love by which we love Christ come first in us, so that by loving Him and doing His commands we deserve to receive the Holy Spirit; and is it *the love,* not of Christ which was already there, but *of God*

in cordibus nostris per Spiritum sanctum, qui datus est nobis?
Perversa est ista sententia. Qui enim se Filium diligere
credit et Patrem non diligit; profecto nec Filium diligit,
sed quod sibi ipse confinxit. Deinde apostolica vox est: *Nemo
dicit Dominus Iesus, nisi in Spiritu sancto* (1 Cor. xii. 3). Et
quis Dominum Iesum, nisi qui eum diligit, dicit, nisi eo modo
dicit, quo Apostolus intelligi voluit? Multi enim voce dicunt,
corde autem et factis negant; sicut de talibus ait: *Confitentur
enim se nosse Deum, factis autem negant* (Tit. i. 16). Si
negatur factis, procul dubio etiam dicitur factis. *Nemo*
itaque *dicit Dominus Iesus* animo, verbo, facto, corde, ore,
opere, *nemo dicit Dominus Iesus, nisi in Spiritu sancto*; et
nemo sic dicit, nisi qui diligit. Iam itaque apostoli dicebant,
Dominus Iesus. Et si eo modo dicebant, ut non ficte dicerent,
ore confitentes, corde et factis negantes; prorsus si veraciter
hoc dicebant, procul dubio diligebant. Quomodo igitur diligebant, nisi in Spiritu sancto? Et tamen eis prius imperatur,
ut diligant eum et eius mandata conservent, ut accipiant
Spiritum sanctum: quem nisi haberent, profecto diligere et
mandata servare non possent.

2. Restat ergo ut intelligamus Spiritum sanctum habere
qui diligit, et habendo mereri ut plus habeat, et plus habendo
plus diligat. Iam itaque habebant Spiritum discipuli, quem
Dominus promittebat, sine quo eum Dominum non dicebant:
nec tamen eum adhuc habebant, sicut eum Dominus promittebat. Et habebant ergo, et non habebant, qui quantum
habendus fuerat, nondum habebant. Habebant itaque minus,
dandus erat eis amplius. Habebant occulte, accepturi fuerant

the Father, that *is shed abroad in our hearts by the Holy Spirit who was given unto us*? That is an utterly false opinion. For he that thinks he loves the Son, and does not love the Father, assuredly does not love the Son, but a fiction of his own devising. Now another Apostolic saying is : *No man saith, Jesus is Lord, but in the Holy Spirit* (1 Cor. xii. 3). And who calls Jesus Lord but him that loves Him, and says the words in the sense in which the Apostle would have his words taken ? Many indeed say the words with their voice, but deny them in heart and deed ; as, speaking of such, he says : *They confess that they know God, but by their deeds deny Him* (Tit. i. 16). Now if deeds deny Him, without doubt deeds also declare Him. *No man*, therefore, *saith, Jesus is Lord*, whether with mind, word, deed, heart, mouth, or work, *no man saith, Jesus is Lord, but in the Holy Spirit* ; and no man saith so but him who loves Him. The Apostles could already say, Jesus is Lord ; and if they so said it that it was not said with feigned intention, the mouth making confession, but heart and deeds denying Him, if in a word they said it sincerely, without doubt they loved Him. How loved they then but in the Holy Spirit ? Yet they are first bidden love Him and keep His commandments in order to receive the Holy Spirit, when, unless they had the Spirit, they certainly could not love and keep commandments.

2.   What therefore we have now to learn is, that he who loves already hath the Holy Spirit, and that his present possession entitles him to a larger possession, and the larger possession tends to a larger love. The disciples already had the Spirit whom the Lord was promising, the Spirit without whom they could not call Him Lord ; but they did not have Him yet as the Lord was promising Him. So they both had and did not have Him, for they had Him not yet in the measure in which He was to be had. They had Him in less measure ; He was to be given in greater measure ; they possessed Him secretly ; they were to receive Him openly ; for the fuller gift

manifeste; quia et hoc ad maius donum sancti Spiritus per-
tinebat, ut eis innotesceret quod habebant. De quo munere
loquens Apostolus ait: *Nos autem non Spiritum huius mundi
accepimus, sed Spiritum qui ex Deo est, ut sciamus quae a
Deo donata sunt nobis* (1 Cor. ii. 12). Nam et ipsam mani-
festam impertitionem Spiritus sancti non semel, sed bis
numero Dominus egit. Mox enim ut resurrexit a mortuis
insufflans ait: *Accipite Spiritum sanctum* (Ioan. xx. 22).
Numquid igitur quia tunc dedit, ideo non misit etiam postea
quem promisit? Aut non idem ipse est Spiritus sanctus, qui
et tunc est insufflatus ab ipso, et postea ab ipso missus e
caelo? Quapropter cur ipsa quae facta est evidenter donatio
eius, bis facta fuerit, alia quaestio est: fortassis enim propter
duo praecepta dilectionis, hoc est proximi et Dei, ut commendaretur ad Spiritum sanctum pertinere dilectio, haec eius
gemina est in manifestatione facta donatio. Et si alia causa
quaerenda est, non nunc eius inquisitione in longiorem quam
oportet modum sermo iste mittendus est: dum tamen constet,
sine Spiritu sancto Christum nos diligere et mandata eius
servare non posse; et id nos posse atque agere tanto minus,
quanto illum percipimus minus; tanto autem amplius, quanto
illum percipimus amplius. Proinde non solum non habenti,
verum etiam habenti non incassum promittitur: non habenti
quidem, ut habeatur; habenti autem, ut amplius habeatur.
Nam nisi ab alio minus, ab alio amplius haberetur, sanctus
Elisaeus sancto Eliae non diceret: *Spiritus qui est in te, duplo
sit in me* (4 Reg. ii. 9).

3. Quando autem ait Ioannes Baptista: *Non enim ad
mensuram dat Deus Spiritum* (Ioan. iii. 34), de ipso Dei Filio
loquebatur, cui non est datus Spiritus ad mensuram; *quia
in illo inhabitat omnis plenitudo Divinitatis* (Coloss. ii. 9).
Neque enim sine gratia Spiritus sancti est *mediator Dei et
hominum homo Christus Iesus* (1 Tim. ii. 5): nam et ipse

of the Holy Spirit consisted partly in the fuller knowledge of
the gift they already had.   The Apostle is speaking of that
fuller gift when he saith : *Now we have received, not the spirit
of this world, but the Spirit who is of God, that we may know
the things which are given us of God* (1 Cor. ii. 12).   Now
even the open imparting of the Holy Spirit by the Lord took
place not once but twice.   For soon after, when He was risen
from the dead, He breathed on them and said : *Receive ye the
Holy Ghost* (Jn. xx. 22).   Because He gave Him then, did He
therefore fail to send anon Him whom He promised ?   Is He
not one and the self-same Holy Spirit, who then was breathed
on them by Him, and later sent by Him from heaven ?   Thus
another question arises, why the gift of the Spirit, which was
manifestly made, was made twice over ; it may be that this
twofold open gift of Him was made on account of the two
commands of love, towards our neighbour and to God, that
love might be proclaimed as belonging to the Holy Spirit.
There may be yet another reason to examine ; but the search
for it must not draw out this present sermon longer than is
meet ; enough that we admit that we cannot love Christ and
keep His commandments without the Holy Spirit ; that this
we can do, and we do, in less or larger degree according
as we receive Him in less or larger measure.   And therefore
He is not idly promised to him that already hath as well as to
him that hath not ; to the latter as a gift, to the former as
the increase of a gift.   For if He were not possessed by one
in less and by another in larger measure, holy Elisha would
not have said to holy Elijah : *Let the Spirit that is in thee rest
on me in double measure* (2 Ki. ii. 9).

    3.   But when John Baptist saith : *For God giveth not
the Spirit by measure* (Jn. iii. 34), he was speaking of the
Son of God Himself, to whom the Spirit was not given by
measure, *because in Him dwelleth all the fulness of the Godhead* (Col. ii. 9), nor yet is He *the Mediator between God and
men, the man Christ Jesus* (1 Tim. ii. 5), without the grace

dicit de se fuisse propheticum illud impletum : *Spiritus
Domini super me; propter quod unxit me, evangelizare
pauperibus misit me* (Isai. lxi. 1; Luc. iv. 18—21). Quod
enim est Unigenitus aequalis Patri, non est gratiae, sed
naturae: quod autem in unitatem personae Unigeniti assumptus
est homo, gratiae est, non naturae, confitente Evangelio atque
dicente: *Puer autem crescebat et confortabatur plenus sapientia, et gratia Dei erat in illo* (Luc. ii. 40). Ceteris autem ad
mensuram datur et datus additur, donec unicuique pro modo
suae perfectionis propria mensura compleatur. Unde et
monet Apostolus, *non plus sapere quam oportet sapere, sed
sapere ad temperantiam, unicuique sicut Deus partitus est
mensuram fidei* (Rom. xii. 3). Neque enim ipse dividitur
Spiritus, sed dona per Spiritum: nam *divisiones donationum
sunt, idem autem Spiritus* (1 Cor. xii. 4).

4. Quod vero ait: *Rogabo Patrem, et alium Paracletum
dabit vobis* (Ioan. xiv. 16), ostendit et se ipsum esse Paracletum.
Paracletus enim latine dicitur advocatus; et dictum est de
Christo : *Advocatum habemus ad Patrem, Iesum Christum
iustum* (1 Ioan. ii. 1). Sic autem mundum dixit non posse
accipere Spiritum sanctum, sicut etiam dictum est: *Prudentia
carnis inimica est in Deum, legi enim Dei non est subiecta, nec
enim potest* (Rom. viii. 7): velut si dicamus, Iniustitia iusta
esse non potest. Mundum quippe ait hoc loco, mundi significans dilectores, *quae* dilectio *non est a Patre* (1 Ioan. ii. 16).
Et ideo dilectioni huius mundi, de qua satis agimus ut minu-
atur et consumatur in nobis, contraria est *dilectio Dei quae
diffunditur in cordibus nostris per Spiritum sanctum, qui
datus est nobis* (Rom. v. 5). *Mundus* ergo *eum accipere non
potest, quia non videt eum, neque scit eum.* Non enim habet

of the Holy Spirit; for He Himself said that the prophetic word was fulfilled in Him: *The Spirit of the Lord is upon me; because He hath anointed Me, He hath sent me to preach the Gospel to the poor* (Is. lxi. 1; Lu. iv. 18—21). That He is the Only-begotten, equal to the Father, is not of grace, but of nature; the taking up of man into the unity of the Person of the Only-begotten, is of grace, not of nature, as the Gospel witnesses and says: *But the child grew and waxed strong, filled with wisdom; and the grace of God was in Him* (Lu. ii. 40). But to the rest of men He is given by measure, and when once given, is given in greater measure, until everyone according to the measure of his perfection hath his proper measure filled up. Wherefore also the Apostle warneth everyone *not to think of himself more highly than he ought to think; but to think soberly, according as God hath dealt to every man the measure of faith* (Rom. xii. 3). The Spirit Himself of course is not divided, but only the gifts bestowed by Him; for *there are divisions of gifts, but the same Spirit* (1 Cor. xii. 4).

4. On the other hand by saying: *I will ask the Father, and He will give you another Paraclete* (Jn. xiv. 16), He shews that He Himself is a Paraclete. Paraclete is the Latin "advocate," and advocate is applied to Christ: *We have an Advocate with the Father, Jesus Christ the righteous* (1 Jn. ii. 1). Now the world cannot, He says, receive the Holy Spirit for the reason conveyed in the text: *The mind of the flesh is at enmity with God; for it is not subject to the Law of God, neither indeed can be* (Rom. viii. 7); in other words, unrighteousness cannot be righteous. By "world" in this place He means of course lovers of the world, *which* love *is not of the Father* (1 Jn. ii. 16). And therefore *the love of God which is shed abroad in our hearts by the Holy Spirit which was given unto us* (Rom. v. 5) is contrary to the love of this world which we are striving to have reduced and utterly removed from our hearts. *The world* then *cannot receive Him, because it seeth Him not, neither knoweth Him.* The love of

invisibiles oculos mundana dilectio, per quos videri Spiritus
sanctus nisi invisibiliter non potest.

5. *Vos autem*, inquit, *cognoscetis eum, quia apud vos
manebit et in vobis erit.* Erit in eis ut maneat, non manebit
ut sit: prius est enim esse alicubi, quam manere. Sed ne
putarent quod dictum est, *apud vos manebit*, ita dictum quemadmodum apud hominem hospes visibiliter manere consuevit,
exposuit quid dixerit, *apud vos manebit*, cum adiunxit et dixit,
in vobis erit. Ergo invisibiliter videtur: nec si non sit in
nobis, potest esse in nobis eius scientia. Sic enim a nobis
videtur in nobis et nostra conscientia: nam faciem videmus
alterius, nostram videre non possumus; conscientiam vero
nostram videmus, alterius non videmus. Sed conscientia nus-
quam est, nisi in nobis: Spiritus autem sanctus potest esse
etiam sine nobis; datur quippe ut sit et in nobis. Sed videri
et sciri quemadmodum videndus et sciendus est, non potest a
nobis, si non sit in nobis.

TRACTATUS LXXV.

De eo quod ait Iesus: *Non relinquam vos orphanos*, usque
     ad id: *Et ego diligam eum, et manifestabo ei me ipsum*
     (xiv. 18—21).

1. Post promissionem Spiritus sancti, ne quisquam
putaret, quod ita eum Dominus daturus fuerat velut pro se
ipso, ut non et ipse cum eis esset futurus, adiecit atque ait:
Non relinquam vos orphanos, veniam ad vos. Orphani,
pupilli sunt. Illud enim graecum eiusdem rei nomen est, hoc
latinum: nam in Psalmo ubi legimus: *Pupillo tu eris adiutor*

the world hath not invisible eyes, by which alone the Holy Spirit can be invisibly beheld.

5. *But ye*, He saith, *shall know Him, for He shall dwell with you and shall be in you.* He shall be in them in order to dwell, not dwell in them in order to be, for being in any place is prior to dwelling in it. But to prevent their thinking that the words *shall dwell with you* were spoken in the usual sense in which we speak of a guest visibly dwelling with a man, He explained what He meant by, *shall dwell with you,* by going on to say, *shall be in you.* Therefore He is seen, though not with visible eyes; nor can the knowledge of Him be in us, if He be not in us Himself. Just in the same way is our conscience seen by us to be within us; for we see our neighbour's face, but not our own; but we see our own conscience, not our neighbour's. But conscience is nowhere but within us, while the Holy Spirit can also be apart from us; indeed He is given that He may be in us as well as without us. But if He be not in us, He cannot be seen and known by us as He ought to be.

HOMILY LXXV.

From Jesus' words, *I will not leave you orphans,* as far as, *And I will love him, and will manifest Myself to him* (xiv. 18—21).

1. After the promise of the Holy Spirit, lest any should think that the Lord was about to give Him as a kind of substitute for Himself, and would not likewise Himself be present with them, He added, *I will not leave you orphans, I will come unto you.* Ὀρφανοί (the fatherless) we call *pupilli.* The one is the Greek, the other the Latin name for the same thing; thus in the Psalm where we read *Pupillo, Thou wilt be a helper*

(Psal. ix. 14), graecus habet orphano. Quamvis ergo nos Filius Dei suo Patri adoptaverit filios, et eundem Patrem nos voluerit habere per gratiam, qui eius Pater est per naturam; tamen etiam ipse circa nos paternum affectum quodam modo demonstrat, cum dicit, *Non relinquam vos orphanos, veniam ad vos.* Hinc est quod etiam sponsi filios nos appellat, ubi dicit: *Veniet hora ut auferatur ab eis sponsus, et tunc ieiunabunt filii sponsi* (Matth. ix. 15). Quis autem sponsus, nisi Dominus Christus?

2. Deinde sequitur et dicit: *Adhuc modicum, et mundus me iam non videt* (Ioan. xiv. 19). Quid enim, tunc eum videbat mundus? quandoquidem mundi nomine vult intelligi eos, de quibus superius est locutus, dicens de Spiritu sancto: *Quem mundus accipere non potest, quia non videt eum neque cognoscit eum* (ib. xiv. 17). Videbat eum plane mundus carneis oculis in carne conspicuum, non autem videbat quod in carne Verbum latebat; videbat hominem, non videbat Deum; videbat indumentum, non videbat indutum. Sed quoniam post resurrectionem etiam ipsam carnem suam, quam non solum videndam, verum etiam contrectandam demonstravit suis, noluit demonstrare non suis; hinc fortasse intelligendum est esse dictum: *Adhuc modicum, et mundus me iam non videt: vos autem videbitis me; quia ego vivo, et vos vivetis.*

3. Quid est, *quia ego vivo, et vos vivetis?* Cur de praesenti se dixit vivere, illos autem de futuro esse victuros, nisi quia vitam etiam carnis utique resurgentis, qualis in ipso praecedebat, et illis est pollicitus secuturam? Et quia ipsius mox futura erat resurrectio, praesentis posuit temporis verbum propter significandam celeritatem: illorum autem quoniam seculi differtur in finem, non ait vivitis, sed *vivetis.* Duas ergo resurrectiones, suam scilicet mox futuram et nostram in

to the fatherless (Ps. x. 14), the Greek has ὀρφανῷ. Although
then the Son of God has made us the adopted sons of His
Father, and hath willed that we should have Him for our
Father by grace who is His Father by nature, yet in saying:
I will not leave you fatherless, I will come to you, He Himself
shews a kind of fatherly feeling towards us. Hence it is that
He also calls us sons of the Bridegroom, saying: *The hour
shall come that the Bridegroom shall be taken from them, and
then shall the sons of the Bridegroom fast* (Mt. ix. 15). Now
who is the Bridegroom but the Lord Christ?

2. Then He goes on to say: *Yet a little while and the
world seeth Me no more* (Jn. xiv. 19). What? did the world
at that time see Him? I ask. Now by the world He means
those of whom He spoke above, when concerning the Holy
Spirit He said: *Whom the world cannot receive, because it
seeth Him not, neither knoweth Him* (ib. xiv. 17). Yes, the
world did see Him then with the eyes of flesh, in flesh made
manifest; it did not see the Word which lay concealed beneath
the flesh; it saw the Man, but not the God; it saw the
clothing, but not Him whom it clothed. But since after the
Resurrection He would not shew to them that were not His that
flesh of His which He did shew to His disciples, ay and let them
see and handle; this was perhaps the cause to which we must
assign the words: *Yet a little while and the world seeth Me no
more: but ye shall see Me; because I live, ye shall live also.*

3. What meaneth, *Because I live, ye shall live also*? Why
did He speak of life as something present for Him, and as
future for them, except as promising that a life of flesh, a risen
flesh, should presently be theirs, of the same kind as that of
which He gave the first example? And because His own
Resurrection was so soon to take place, He used a verb in the
present tense in order to signify its swift approach; but since
theirs is deferred till the end of the world, He saith not, ye
live, but *ye shall live.* It was then the promise of two resur-
rections, viz. His own immediate one, and ours which will

5—2

seculi fine venturam, duobus verbis praesentis temporis et
futuri eleganter breviterque promisit. *Quia ego*, inquit, *vivo,
et vos vivetis* : quia ille vivit, ideo et nos vivemus. *Per
hominem quippe mors, et per hominem resurrectio mortuorum.
Sicut enim in Adam omnes moriuntur, sic in Christo omnes
vivificabuntur* (1 Cor. xv. 21, 22). Quoniam nemo ad mortem
nisi per illum, nemo ad vitam nisi per Christum. Quia nos*
viximus, mortui sumus: quia vivit ipse, vivemus nos. Mortui
sumus illi, quando viximus nobis : quia vero mortuus ille
pro nobis, et sibi vivit et nobis. Quia enim vivit ille, et nos
vivemus. Nam sicut per nos mortem habere potuimus, non
sic et vitam per nos habere possumus.

4. *In illo die,* inquit, *vos cognoscetis, quia ego sum in
Patre meo, et vos in me, et ego in vobis* (Ioan. xiv. 20). In
quo die, nisi de quo ait: *et vos vivetis* ? Tunc enim erit, ut
possimus videre quod credimus. Nam et nunc est in nobis et
nos in illo: sed hoc nunc credimus, tunc etiam cognoscemus,
quamvis et nunc credendo noverimus, sed tunc contemplando
noscemus. *Quamdiu* enim *sumus in corpore,* quale nunc est,
id est *corruptibile quod aggravat animam, peregrinamur a
Domino: per fidem enim ambulamus, non per speciem* (Sap. ix.
15; 2 Cor. v. 6—8). Tunc ergo per speciem, *quoniam videbimus eum sicuti est* (1 Ioan. iii. 2). Nam si etiam nunc
Christus in nobis non esset, non diceret Apostolus: *Si autem
Christus in nobis, corpus quidem mortuum est propter peccatum, spiritus autem vita est propter iustitiam* (Rom. viii. 10).
Qui vero et nos etiam nunc in illo sumus, satis ostendit, ubi
dicit: *Ego sum vitis, vos palmites* (Ioan. xv. 5). In illo ergo
die, quando vivemus ea vita, qua mors absorbebitur, cognoscemus quia ipse in Patre, et nos in ipso, et ipse in nobis:
quia tunc perficietur hoc ipsum, quod et nunc inchoatum est
iam per ipsum, ut sit in nobis et nos in ipso.

* Editi *nobis.*

ensue at the end of the world, that He correctly and briefly
expressed by two verbs of present and future tense. *Because
I live*, He saith, *ye shall live also*; because He lives, therefore
we shall live also. For *by man came death, and by Man the
resurrection of the dead. For as in Adam all die, so in Christ
shall all be made alive* (1 Cor. xv. 21, 22). Since no man
attains to death except through Adam, so no man attains to
life except through Christ. Life, as we have lived it, must end
in death; His life ensures our life. Dead were we to Him so
long as we lived to ourselves; but because He died for us,
He liveth both to Himself and to us. For because He lives,
we shall live also. Death indeed we have been able by
ourselves to win; we cannot in the same way by ourselves
win life.

4. *In that day*, He saith, *ye shall know that I am in My
Father, and ye in Me, and I in you* (Jn. xiv. 20). In what
day, if not that whereof He said: *ye shall live also*? For then
will it be that we shall be able to see what we believe. For
even now He is in us, and we in Him: but whereas we believe
this now, then we shall also know it; though indeed we know
even now by faith, then we shall know by sight. For *so long
as we are in the body*, such as it now is, i.e. *corruptible, which
weigheth down the soul, we are absent from the Lord; for we
walk by faith, not by sight* (Wisd. ix. 15; 2 Cor. v. 6—8). So
then it will be by sight, *for we shall see Him as He is* (1 Jn. iii.
2). For if Christ were not in us now, the Apostle would not
say: *But if Christ be in us, the body indeed is dead because of
sin, but the Spirit is life because of righteousness* (Rom. viii.
10). But He clearly shews that we are even now in Him by
saying: *I am the Vine, ye are the branches* (Jn. xv. 5). In
that day then when we are living that life in which death
shall be swallowed up, we shall know that He is in the
Father, and we in Him, and He in us; for then shall that be
brought to perfection which is even now begun by Him, viz.
that He should be in us, and we in Him.

5. *Qui habet,* inquit, *mandata mea, et servat ea, ille est qui diligit me* (Ioan. xiv. 21). Qui habet in memoria, et servat in vita; qui habet in sermonibus, et servat in moribus; qui habet audiendo, et servat faciendo; aut qui habet faciendo, et servat perseverando: *ipse est,* inquit, *qui diligit me.* Opere est demonstranda dilectio, ne sit infructuosa nominis appellatio. *Et qui diligit me,* inquit, *diligetur a Patre meo; et ego diligam eum, et manifestabo ei me ipsum.* Quid est *diligam,* tamquam tunc dilecturus sit, et nunc non diligit? Absit. Quomodo enim nos Pater sine Filio, aut Filius sine Patre diligeret? Quomodo cum inseparabiliter operentur, separabiliter diligunt? Sed ad hoc dixit, *diligam eum,* ad quod sequitur, *et manifestabo ei me ipsum. Diligam et manifestabo*: id est, ad hoc diligam, ut manifestem. Nunc enim ad hoc dilexit, ut credamus et mandatum fidei teneamus: tunc ad hoc diliget, ut videamus, et ipsam visionem mercedem fidei capiamus. Quia et nos nunc diligimus credendo quod videbimus; tunc autem diligemus, videndo quod credimus.

TRACTATUS LXXVI.

De eo quod sequitur: *Dicit ei Iudas, non ille Iscariotes* etc.,
usque ad id: *Sermo quem audistis non est meus, sed eius
qui misit me Patris* (xiv. 22—24).

1. Interrogantibus discipulis et eis magistro respondente Iesu, etiam nos tamquam cum illis discimus, quando sanctum Evangelium vel legimus vel audimus. Quia ergo dixerat Dominus: *Adhuc modicum, et mundus me iam non videt, vos*

5. *He that hath My commandments,* He saith, *and keepeth them, he it is that loveth Me* (Jn. xiv. 21). He that hath them in mind, and keepeth them in life; he that hath on his tongue, and keepeth in his conduct; he that hath by hearing, and keepeth by doing; or he that hath by doing, and keepeth by perseverance, *he it is that loveth Me.* Love must be proved by works, that it be not a mere barren name. *And he that loveth Me shall be loved of My Father, and I will love him and will manifest Myself unto him.*

Will love? Does this mean that He will love anon, but loves not now? God forbid. How should the Father love us without the Son, or the Son love us without the Father? How can they who are inseparable in work be separable in love? The words, *I will love him,* have the same motive as those which follow : *and I will manifest Myself unto him. I will love, and I will manifest* ; i.e. will love in order that I may manifest. He hath loved us now to the end that we may believe and keep the commandment of faith ; then He will love us to the end that we may see and win the vision itself as the reward of faith. And we too love now by believing that which we shall see, but then we shall love by seeing that which we believe.

HOMILY LXXVI.

From the words next following : *Judas saith unto Him, not Iscariot* etc., as far as, *The word which ye have heard is not Mine, but the Father's who sent Me* (xiv. 22—24).

1. The disciples put their questions, and Jesus their Master answers them, and we also are as it were their fellow-learners, as often as we either read or hear the Holy Gospel. The Lord had said, *Yet a little while, and the world*

autem videbitis me; interrogavit eum de hoc ipso Iudas, non ille traditor eius, qui Iscariotes cognominatus est, sed cuius epistola inter Scripturas canonicas legitur: *Domine, quid factum est, quia nobis manifestaturus es te ipsum, et non mundo?* Simus cum ipsis tamquam interrogantes discipuli, communemque magistrum audiamus et nos. Iudas enim sanctus, non immundus, nec insectator Domini, sed sectator, causam quaesivit, quare se non mundo, sed suis manifestaturus esset Iesus ; quare adhuc modicum et mundus non videret eum, ipsi autem viderent eum.

2. *Respondit Iesus et dixit ei: Si quis diligit me, sermonem meum servabit: et Pater meus diliget eum, et ad eum veniemus, et mansionem apud eum faciemus. Qui non diligit me, sermones meos non servat.* Ecce exposita est causa, quare se suis manifestaturus est, non alienis, quos mundi nomine appellat, et ipsa est causa quod hi diligant, illi non diligant. Ipsa causa est, de qua sacer insonat Psalmus: *Iudica me Deus, et discerne causam meam de gente non sancta* (Psal. xlii. 1). Qui enim diligunt*, quia diligunt, eliguntur ; qui vero non diligunt, *si linguis hominum loquantur et angelorum, fiunt aeramentum sonans et cymbalum tinniens: etsi habuerint prophetiam, et scierint omnia sacramenta, et omnem scientiam, et habuerint omnem fidem ut montes transferant, nihil sunt; etsi distribuerint omnem substantiam suam et tradiderint corpus suum ut ardeant, nihil eis prodest* (1 Cor. xiii. 1—3). Dilectio sanctos discernit a mundo, quae *facit unanimes habitare in domo* (Psal. lxvii. 7). In qua domo facit Pater et Filius mansionem : qui donant et ipsam dilectionem, quibus donent in fine etiam ipsam suam manifestationem: de qua discipulus Magistrum interrogavit, ut non solum illi, qui tunc audiebant per os eius, sed etiam nos per Evangelium eius hoc

* Decem MSS. *diliguntur.*

seeth Me no more, but ye shall see Me. Judas accordingly asked His meaning—not that Judas who betrayed Him and whose surname was Iscariot, but he whose epistle is read among the Canonical Scriptures : *Lord, what has come to pass that Thou wilt manifest Thyself unto us, and not unto the world?* Let us place ourselves beside them like questioning disciples, and hear our common Master. Judas, not the sinner, but the saint, not the Lord's pursuer, but His follower, asked the reason why Jesus would manifest Himself to His own, but not unto the world ; why, yet a little while, and the world should see Him not, but they should see Him ?

2. *Jesus answered and said unto him, If a man love Me, he will keep My word ; and My Father will love him, and We will come unto him, and make Our abode with him. He that loveth Me not keepeth not My sayings.* Lo, here we have set forth to us the cause why He will manifest Himself to His own, and not to aliens, whom He calls "the world," and the cause is just this, that the former love, the latter love Him not. It is the very cause of which the sacred psalmist cries : *Judge me, O God, and decide my cause against an unholy people* (Ps. xliii. 1). For they that love are chosen because they love ; but they that love not, *though they speak with the tongues of men and of angels, become sounding brass and a tinkling cymbal : though they have prophecy and know all mysteries and all knowledge, and have all faith so that they can remove mountains, they are nothing ; though they bestow abroad all their goods, and though they give their body to be burned, it profiteth them nothing* (1 Cor. xiii. 1—3).

Love keeps saints separate from the world ; love which *maketh men to dwell with one mind in an house* (Ps. lxviii. 6), in which house the Father and the Son make their abode ; who give that very love to those to whom in the end they mean to give the promised manifestation of themselves ; concerning which the disciple asked the Master, that not only they might know it who heard it from His lips, but we too

nosse possemus. Quaesierat enim de Christi manifestatione,
et audivit de dilectione atque mansione. Est ergo quaedam
Dei manifestatio interior, quam prorsus impii non noverunt,
quibus Dei Patris et Spiritus sancti manifestatio nulla est:
Filii vero potuit esse, sed in carne; quae nec talis est qualis
illa, nec semper illis adesse potest, qualiscunque sit, sed ad
modicum tempus; et hoc ad iudicium, non ad gaudium; ad
supplicium, non ad praemium.

3. Nunc est ergo ut intelligamus, quantum aperire ipse
dignatur, quomodo dictum sit: *Adhuc modicum, et mundus
me iam non videt, vos autem videbitis me.* Verum est quidem,
quod post paululum etiam corpus suum, in quo poterant eum
et impii videre, oculis eorum fuerat subtracturus: quandoquidem post resurrectionem nemo illorum vidit eum. Sed
quoniam dictum est testantibus angelis: *Sic veniet quemadmodum vidistis eum euntem in caelum* (Act. i. 11): nec aliud
credimus quam eum in eodem corpore ad iudicium vivorum
et mortuorum esse venturum: procul dubio tunc eum videbit
mundus, quo nomine significati sunt a regno eius alieni. Ac
per hoc longe melius intelligitur iam illud tempus significare
voluisse, in eo quod ait: *Adhuc modicum et mundus me iam
non videt,* quando in fine seculi auferetur ab oculis damna-
torum, ut illi eum de cetero videant, apud quos diligentes
eum facit Pater atque ipse mansionem. *Modicum* autem dixit,
quia et id quod prolixum videtur hominibus, brevissimum est
ante oculos Dei: de hoc quippe modico iste ipse Ioannes
evangelista: *Filioli,* inquit, *novissima hora est* (1 Ioan. ii.
18).

4. Ne quis porro existimet Patrem tantummodo et
Filium sine Spiritu sancto apud dilectores suos facere man-

who hear it from His Gospel. He had asked concerning the manifestation of Christ; the answer told him also of Christ's loving and abiding. There is then a certain inner manifestation of God, all unknown to the ungodly, who receive no manifestation of God the Father and the Holy Spirit; that of the Son alone is possible for them, and of Him only in the flesh; a manifestation quite unlike the other, and one which, such as it is, is able to abide with them not for ever, but only for a little while, bringing judgment and not joy, punishment and not reward.

3. Our present task then is to understand, so far as He deigns to disclose it, the meaning of this utterance of the Lord: *Yet a little while, and the world seeth Me no more, but ye shall see Me.* It is quite true that after a brief space He was in fact to withdraw His Body, in which He was visible even to the ungodly, from their sight—since none of them saw Him after the Resurrection. But since it was declared by angel witnesses: *He shall so come in like manner as ye have seen Him go into heaven* (Acts i. 11), and we believe naught else but that He will come in that same body to judge the quick and the dead; there is no doubt that then the world— by which is meant the aliens from His kingdom—will see Him. It is therefore far better to understand that when He said: *Yet a little while, and the world seeth Me no more,* He was already pointing to that time, when in the end of the world He shall be taken from the eyes of the damned to be seen henceforth by those with whom, because they love Him, the Father and Himself will make their dwelling. He said, *a little while,* because what seemeth long drawn out to men is in God's eyes but very brief; and doubtless it is this little while to which our writer John the Evangelist refers in saying: *Children, it is the last hour* (1 Jn. ii. 18).

4. Now if any man begins to think that the Father only and the Son, without the Holy Spirit, make their dwelling with the loving soul, let him remember what has been said

sionem, recolat quod superius de Spiritu sancto dictum est:
*Quem mundus non potest accipere, quia non videt eum, nec scit
eum: vos autem cognoscetis eum, quia apud vos manebit, et in
vobis erit.* Ecce facit in sanctis cum Patre et Filio sanctus
etiam Spiritus mansionem; intus utique tamquam Deus in
templo suo. Deus Trinitas, Pater et Filius et Spiritus sanctus,
veniunt ad nos, dum venimus ad eos: veniunt subveniendo,
venimus obediendo; veniunt illuminando, venimus intuendo:
veniunt implendo, venimus capiendo: ut sit nobis eorum non
extraria visio, sed interna; et in nobis eorum non transitoria
mansio, sed aeterna. Sic mundo non se Filius manifestat:
mundus enim dictus est hoc loco, de quibus continuo subiunxit: *Qui non diligit me, sermones meos non servat.* Hi
sunt qui Patrem et Spiritum sanctum nunquam vident:
Filium autem non ut beatificentur, sed ut iudicentur, ad
modicum vident; nec ipsum in forma Dei, ubi est cum Patre
et Spiritu sancto pariter invisibilis, sed in forma hominis,
ubi esse voluit mundo patiendo contemptibilis, iudicando
terribilis.

5. Quod vero adiunxit: *Et sermo quem audistis non est
meus, sed eius qui misit me Patris*; non miremur, non paveamus: non est minor Patre, sed non est nisi a Patre; non
est impar ipso, sed non est a se ipso. Neque enim mentitus
est dicendo: *Qui non diligit me, sermones meos non servat.*
Ecce suos dixit esse sermones; numquid sibi ipse est con-
trarius, ubi rursus dixit: *Et sermo quem audistis non est meus?*
Et fortasse propter aliquam distinctionem, ubi suos dixit, dixit
pluraliter, hoc est *sermones;* ubi autem *sermonem,* hoc est
Verbum, non suum dixit esse, sed Patris, se ipsum intelligi

already concerning the Holy Spirit : *Whom the world cannot receive, because it seeth Him not, neither knoweth Him: but ye shall know Him, for He shall dwell with you, and shall be in you.* Yea, the Holy Spirit also makes His house with holy men, together with the Father and the Son; within them rather, as God within His temple. God the Trinity, Father, Son, and Holy Spirit come to us, even while we come to them; they come by answering our call, we by obeying theirs; they come by giving light, we by employing sight; they come by filling us with themselves, we come by being filled by them; and thus our vision of them is not external but internal, and their abiding within us is not for a passing while but for eternity. The Son manifests not Himself after this fashion unto the world, for "world" is here used of them concerning whom He straightway added : *He that loveth Me not, keepeth not My sayings.* These are they who never see the Father and the Holy Spirit; the Son indeed they do see for a little while, not to be blessed, but to be judged by Him; yet even Him they see not in the Form of God wherein He is with Father and with Holy Spirit alike invisible, but in the form of man alone, wherein He has willed to be the object of the world's contempt in His suffering, and of its terror in the execution of His judgment.

5. He further added : *And the word which ye have heard is not Mine, but the Father's who sent Me.* This must not raise our wonder or our fear; He is not less than the Father, but He is only of the Father; He is not His inferior, but His being is not of Himself. For He spake no untruth when He said, *He that loveth Me not, keepeth not My words.* He called them *His* words. Does He then contradict Himself, when again He saith : *And the word which ye have heard, is not Mine?* And it may have been to mark a real distinction that where He called them His, He used the plural number "words," but where He said that the utterance, that is the Word, was not His but the Father's, He meant Himself.

voluit. *In principio* enim *erat Verbum, et Verbum erat apud
Deum, et Deus erat Verbum* (Ioan. i. 1). Non utique suum,
sed Patris est Verbum: quomodo nec sua imago, sed Patris;
nec suus Filius idem ipse, sed Patris. Recte igitur tribuit
auctori quidquid facit aequalis, a quo habet hoc ipsum quod
illi est indifferenter aequalis.

TRACTATUS LXXVII.

De eo quod sequitur: *Haec locutus sum vobis apud vos manens,*
usque ad id: *Pacem meam do vobis, non quomodo mundus
dat, ego do vobis* (xiv. 25—27).

1. In praecedenti lectione sancti Evangelii, quam sequitur
ista, quae modo recitata est, Dominus Iesus dixerat se et
Patrem ad dilectores suos esse venturos, et apud eos mansionem esse facturos. Iamvero et superius dixerat de Spiritu
sancto: *Vos autem cognoscetis eum, quia apud vos manebit, et
in vobis erit* (Ioan. xiv. 17): unde intelleximus in sanctis
tamquam in templo suo simul manere Trinitatem Deum.
Nunc autem dicit: *Haec locutus sum vobis apud vos manens.*
Illa itaque mansio alia est quam promisit futuram, haec vero
alia quam praesentem esse testatur. Illa spiritalis est atque
intrinsecus mentibus redditur; haec corporalis forinsecus
oculis atque auribus exhibetur. Illa in aeternum beatificat
liberatos; haec in tempore visitat liberandos. Secundum illam
Dominus a suis dilectoribus non recedit; secundum hanc
it et recedit. *Haec,* inquit, *locutus sum vobis, apud vos*

For, *In the beginning was the Word, and the Word was with God, and the Word was God* (Jn. i. 1). He verily is not His own Word, but the Father's, as He is not His own Image, but the Father's, or His own Son, but the Father's. It is right of Him therefore to assign whatever He, the co-equal, doeth, to the Author from whom He hath this very attribute, to be without distinction equal unto Him.

HOMILY LXXVII.

From what follows next, *These things have I spoken unto you, while yet abiding with you,* as far as, *My Peace I give unto you : not as the world giveth, give I unto you* (xiv. 25—27).

1. In the lection of the Holy Gospel immediately preceding that which has just been read, the Lord Jesus had said that He and the Father would come to them that love Him, and make their abode with them. Now He had already in an earlier passage said concerning the Holy Spirit : *But ye shall know Him, for He shall dwell with you, and shall be in you* (Jn. xiv. 17); by which we understood that God the Trinity dwells together in the saints as in His own temple. Now however He saith : *These things have I spoken to you, while yet abiding with you.* Thus there are two kinds of abiding, one which He promised in the future, the other which He declares to be already present. The former is spiritual, granted inwardly to the mind ; the latter corporeal, presented outwardly to eye and ear. The former gives bliss for all eternity to them that are delivered ; the latter pays a visit in time to those that are heirs of deliverance. The former suffers not the Lord to return from the souls that love Him, the latter lets Him go and return. *These things have I spoken*

manens: utique praesentia corporali, qua cum illis visibilis loquebatur.

2. *Paracletus autem,* inquit, *Spiritus sanctus, quem mittet Pater in nomine meo, ille vos docebit omnia, et commemorabit vos omnia, quaecunque dixero vobis* (Ioan. xiv. 26). Numquidnam dicit Filius et docet Spiritus sanctus, ut dicente Filio verba capiamus, docente autem Spiritu sancto eadem verba intelligamus? Quasi dicat Filius sine Spiritu sancto, aut Spiritus sanctus doceat sine Filio: aut vero non et Filius doceat et Spiritus sanctus dicat, et cum Deus aliquid dicit et docet, Trinitas ipsa dicat et doceat? Sed quoniam Trinitas est, oportebat eius singulas insinuare personas, eamque nos distincte audire, inseparabiliter intelligere. Audi Patrem dicentem ubi legis: *Dominus dixit ad me, Filius meus es tu* (Psal. ii. 7); audi et docentem ubi legis: *Omnis qui audivit a Patre et didicit, venit ad me* (Ioan. vi. 45). Filium vero dicentem modo audisti, de se quippe ait: *Quaecunque dixero vobis;* quem si et docentem vis nosse, magistrum recole: *Unus est,* inquit, *magister vester Christus* (Matth. xxiii. 10). Spiritum porro sanctum, quem modo audisti docentem ubi dictum est: *Ipse vos docebit omnia,* audi etiam dicentem, ubi legis in Actibus apostolorum beato Petro dixisse Spiritum sanctum: *Vade cum illis, quia ego misi eos* (Act. x. 20). Omnis igitur et dicit et docet Trinitas, sed nisi etiam singillatim commendaretur, eam nullo modo humana capere utique posset infirmitas. Cum ergo omnino sit inseparabilis, nunquam Trinitas esse sciretur, si semper inseparabiliter diceretur: nam et cum dicimus Patrem et Filium et Spiritum sanctum, non eos utique

unto you, He says, *while yet abiding with you* ; abiding in that corporeal presence in which they saw Him while He was speaking with them.

2. *But the Paraclete,* He says, *the Holy Spirit, whom the Father will send in My Name, He shall teach you all things, and bring all things to your remembrance, whatsoever I have said unto you* (Jn. xiv. 26). How? Doth the Son speak and the Holy Spirit teach? Is it the case that the Words which fall to us when the Son speaks, are explained to us by the teaching of the Holy Spirit? As though the Son could speak without the Holy Spirit, or the Holy Spirit teach without the Son, and the truth were not this, that both the Son teaches and the Holy Spirit speaks, and that when God speaks and teaches anything, it is the Trinity that speaks and teaches. But being Trinity, it was necessary to introduce the Persons severally, that therein we might both perceive distinctions and recognise inseparable unity. Listen to the Father speaking when thou readest: *The Lord said unto Me, Thou art My Son* (Ps. ii. 7). Hear Him also teaching when thou readest: *Every man that hath heard of the Father and hath learned, cometh unto Me* (Jn. vi. 45). Thou hast this instant heard the Son speaking, for concerning Himself He saith: *Whatsoever I have said unto you;* if thou wouldst also know that He teacheth, remember the word " Master." *One,* saith He, *is your Master, even Christ* (Mt. xxiii. 10). Yea and the Holy Spirit, whom thou just now heardest to be teacher from the words, *He shall teach you all things,* doth also speak, as thou must learn from reading in the Acts of the Apostles that He spake to blessed Peter, *Go with them, for I have sent them* (Acts x. 20). Hence all the Trinity both speaks and teaches, but unless It were presented to us Person by Person, human weakness would be utterly unable to conceive It. Thus being as It is a quite indivisible Unity, It could never be known as a Trinity, if It were always spoken of undividedly ; for even when we speak of Father, Son, and Holy Spirit, we do not in

dicimus simul, cum ipsi non possint esse non simul. Quod vero addidit, *commemorabit vos*, intelligere debemus etiam, quod iubemur non oblivisci, saluberrimos monitus ad gratiam pertinere, quam nos commemorat Spiritus.

3. *Pacem,* inquit, *relinquo vobis, pacem meam do vobis.* Hoc est quod legimus apud Prophetam : *Pacem super pacem* (Isai. lvii. 17); pacem nobis relinquit iturus, pacem suam nobis dabit in fine venturus. Pacem nobis relinquit in hoc saeculo, pacem suam nobis dabit in futuro saeculo. Pacem suam nobis relinquit, in qua manentes hostem vincimus : pacem suam nobis dabit, quando sine hoste regnabimus. Pacem relinquit nobis, ut etiam hic invicem diligamus : pacem suam nobis dabit, ubi nunquam dissentire possimus. Pacem relinquit nobis, ne de occultis nostris invicem iudicemus, cum in hoc sumus mundo : pacem suam dabit nobis, cum *manifestabit cogitationes cordis, et tunc laus erit unicuique a Deo* (1 Cor. iv. 5). In illo tamen atque ab illo nobis est pax, sive quam nobis relinquit iturus ad Patrem, sive quam nobis dabit nos perducturus ad Patrem. Quid autem nobis relinquit ascendens a nobis, nisi se ipsum, dum non recedit a nobis ? *Ipse est enim pax nostra, qui fecit utraque unum* (Ephes. ii. 14). Pax ergo ipse nobis est, et cum credimus quia est, et cum videmus eum sicuti est. Si enim *quamdiu sumus in corpore corruptibili quod aggravat animam* (Sap. ix. 15), cum *per fidem ambulamus non per speciem,* non deserit *peregrinantes a se* (2 Cor. v. 6, 7) : quanto magis cum ad ipsam speciem venerimus, nos implebit ex se ?

4. Sed quid est quod ubi ait : *Pacem relinquo vobis,* non addidit *meam :* ubi vero ait *do vobis,* ibi dixit *meam* ? Utrum subaudiendum est *meam,* et ubi dictum non est, quia potest

fact pronounce the Names simultaneously, although the
Persons cannot but be together. But when He added: *He
shall bring to your remembrance,* we ought also to understand
what we are bidden not forget, that every wholesome hint
belongeth to that grace which the Holy Spirit brings to our
remembrance.

3. *Peace,* He says, *I leave with you, My peace I give unto
you.* This is what we read in the Prophet: *Peace upon
peace* (Is. lvii. 19). Peace He leaves us at His going, His
peace He will give us in the end at His coming. Peace
He leaves with us in this world, His peace He will give us
in the world to come. His peace He leaves us, by abiding in
which we overcome the enemy; His peace He will give us,
when we shall reign without a foe to fear. Peace He leaves
us that we may love each other even on earth; His peace He
will give us in that place where we can never be at variance.
Peace He leaves us, that while we are in this world we may not
judge one another for our secret faults; His peace He will
give us, when *He shall make manifest the thoughts of the heart,
and then shall every man have praise of God* (1 Cor. iv. 5).
Yet in Him and from Him have we our peace, whether that
peace which He leaves us when He goeth to the Father, or
that which He will give us when He shall lead us to the
Father. But what does He leave us, when ascending from us,
but His own self, seeing that He departs not from us? *For
He is our peace, who hath made both one* (Eph. ii. 14). He
Himself then is our peace, both when we believe that He is,
and when we see Him as He is. For if *while we are in the
body of corruption which weigheth down the soul* (Wisd. ix. 15),
and *walk by faith and not by sight,* He deserteth not *those that
are absent from Him* (2 Cor. v. 6, 7); shall He not much more
fill us with Himself, when we come to see Him as He is?

4. But why, in the phrase: *Peace I leave with you,* did He
omit the *My,* whereas in, *I give to you,* He added it? Are we
to supply *My* even where it is not said, on the ground that

referri ad utrumque etiam quod semel dictum est ? An forte
et hic aliquid latet quod petendum est et quaerendum, et ad
quod pulsantibus aperiendum ? Quid si enim pacem suam
eam voluit intelligi qualem habet ipse ? Pax vero ista quam
nobis relinquit in hoc saeculo, nostra est potius dicenda quam
ipsius. Ille quippe nihil repugnat in se ipso, qui nullum
habet omnino peccatum; nos autem talem pacem nunc
habemus, in qua adhuc dicamus : *Dimitte nobis debita nostra*
(Matth. vi. 12). Est ergo nobis pax aliqua, *quoniam conde-
lectamur legi Dei secundum interiorem hominem* : sed non est
plena, quia videmus *aliam legem in membris* nostris *repug-
nantem legi mentis* nostrae (Rom. vii. 22, 23). Itemque inter
nos ipsos est nobis pax, quia invicem nobis credimus quod
invicem diligamus : sed nec ipsa plena est, quia cogitationes
cordis nostri invicem non videmus; et quaedam de nobis,
quae non sunt in nobis, vel in melius invicem vel in deterius
opinamur. Itaque ista, etiamsi ab illo nobis relicta est, pax
nostra est : nisi enim ab illo, non haberemus et talem, sed
ipse non habet talem. Si tenuerimus usque in finem qualem
accepimus, qualem habet habebimus, ubi nihil nobis repugnet
ex nobis, et nihil nos invicem lateat in cordibus nostris. Nec
ignoro ista Domini verba etiam sic accipi posse, ut eiusdem
sententiae repetitio videatur, *Pacem relinquo vobis, pacem
meam do vobis* : ut quod dixerat *pacem,* hoc repetierit dicens
pacem meam; et quod dixerat *relinquo vobis,* hoc repetierit
dicens *do vobis.* Ut volet quisque accipiat : me tamen delectat,
credo et vos, fratres mei dilecti, sic tenere istam pacem, ubi
adversarium concorditer vincimus, ut desideremus pacem, ubi
adversarium non habebimus.

5. Quod vero Dominus adiunxit atque ait : *Non quomodo*

having been used in one place it may refer to both? Or is there perchance something hidden here as well, which we must ask and seek, and which is to be opened to those that knock at it? What if by His peace He meant the peace He hath Himself? And truly the present peace He leaves us in this world is rather to be called our peace than His. He is never at war within Himself, because He is quite free from sin; but the peace which we have hitherto is such that in the midst of it we must still say: *Forgive us our debts* (Mt. vi. 12). And so we have a kind of peace, *since we delight in the law of God after the inner man*; but this is not a perfect peace, because we *see another law in* our *members, warring against the law of* our *mind* (Rom. vii. 22, 23). And in like manner we have peace among ourselves, because we mutually believe that we have mutual love; but neither is this a perfect peace, because we do not see into one another's thought and heart; and some things we surmise concerning ourselves which are not in us, when we think too well, or else too ill, one of another. And so this peace, although it hath been left to us by Him, is still our peace; for were it not from Him, we should not even have it such as it is; but such is not the peace He hath. If we hold to the end the peace we have received, we shall have the peace that He has, where nothing from within us can make war against us, and no secrets in our hearts can be hidden from our neighbour. I know of course that these words of the Lord can also so be taken as to seem a repetition of the same idea: *Peace I leave with you, My peace I give unto you*; so that when He said *My peace*, He just repeated *peace*; that when He said, *I give unto you*, He merely meant, *I leave unto you*. Let each one take it as he will; but what I like, and what I think you like, beloved brethren, is so to hold the peace we have, wherein in unity of heart we overcome the foe, as still to long for the peace where there shall be no longer any foe to fear.

5. But He went on to say: *Not as the world giveth,*

mundus dat, ego do vobis : quid est aliud, nisi non quomodo homines dant qui diligunt mundum, ita do vobis ? Qui propterea dant sibi pacem, ut sine molestia litium atque bellorum, non Deo, sed amico suo mundo perfruantur : et quando iustis dant pacem ut non eos persequantur, pax non potest esse vera, ubi non est vera concordia, quia disiuncta sunt corda. Quomodo enim consors dicitur, qui sortem iungit : ita ille concors dicendus est, qui corda iungit. Nos ergo, carissimi, quibus Christus pacem relinquit, et pacem suam nobis dat, non sicut mundus, sed sicut ille per quem factus est mundus, ut concordes simus, iungamus invicem corda, et cor unum sursum habeamus, ne corrumpatur in terra.

TRACTATUS LXXVIII.

In id quod Dominus dicit : *Non turbetur cor vestrum, neque formidet* etc. (xiv. 27, 28).

1. Accepimus, fratres, verba Domini dicentis ad disci-pulos suos : *Non turbetur cor vestrum, neque formidet Audistis quia ego dixi vobis : Vado et venio ad vos : si dilige-retis me, gauderetis utique, quia ego vado ad Patrem ; quia Pater maior me est.* Hinc ergo turbari et formidare poterat cor illorum, quod ibat ab eis, quamvis venturus ad eos : ne forsitan gregem lupus hoc intervallo invaderet, pastoris absentia. Sed a quibus homo abscedebat, Deus non derelin-quebat : et idem ipse Christus homo et Deus. Ergo et ibat per id quod homo erat, et manebat per id quod Deus erat : ibat per id quod uno loco erat, manebat per id quod ubique erat. Cur itaque turbaretur et formidaret cor, quando ita

give I unto you. What else is this but, " Not as men give
who love the world, give I unto you"? They give peace
unto themselves, only that without hindrance of strifes and
wars they may have enjoyment, not of God, but of the world
they love. And even when they so far give the righteous
peace as not to persecute them, yet here there cannot be true
peace, where no true concord is, and heart is not at one with
heart. We say a man *consorteth*, when he joins lot (*sors*) with
lot ; so we may say that he *concordeth*, who joins heart (*cor*)
to heart. Let us then, beloved, to whom Christ leaves peace
and gives His peace, not as the world gives, but as He gives
who made the world : let us join heart to heart, that we may
thus be in concord ; let us lift up our heart, a single heart, to
heaven, that it fall not into corruption here on earth.

HOMILY LXXVIII.

On the Lord's words, *Let not your heart be troubled,
neither let it be afraid* etc. (xiv. 27, 28).

1. We have heard, brethren, the Lord's voice saying to
His disciples : *Let not your heart be troubled, neither let it be
afraid. Ye have heard how I said unto you, I go away and
come again unto you. If ye loved me, ye would surely rejoice
because I go unto the Father ; for the Father is greater
than I.* Their heart might well be troubled and afraid at His
going from them, even though He was to come to them again ;
the wolf was only too likely to attack the flock in this interval
of the Shepherd's absence. But they from whom He went
away as Man were not bereft of Him as God ; and Christ is
Himself at once both Man and God. Thus in that He was
Man He went ; in that He was God He stayed. He went, in
as much as He was in one place ; He abode, in as much
as He was present everywhere. Why then should the heart
be troubled and afraid, since it was the eye only He was

deserebat oculos, ut non desereret cor ? Quamvis Deus etiam qui nullo continetur loco, discedat ab eorum cordibus, qui eum relinquunt moribus, non pedibus ; et veniat ad eos, qui convertuntur ad eum non facie, sed fide, et accedunt ad eum mente, non carne. Ut autem intelligerent secundum id quod homo erat, eum dixisse : *Vado et venio ad vos* ; adiecit atque ait : *Si diligeretis me, gauderetis utique, quia ego vado ad Patrem* ; *quia Pater maior me est.* Per quod ergo Filius non est aequalis Patri, per hoc iturus erat ad Patrem, a quo venturus est vivos iudicaturus et mortuos ; per illud autem in quo aequalis est gignenti Unigenitus, nunquam recedit a Patre, sed cum illo est ubique totus pari divinitate, quam nullus continet locus. *Cum* enim *in forma Dei esset,* sicut Apostolus loquitur, *non rapinam arbitratus est esse aequalis Deo.* Quomodo enim rapina posset esse natura, quae non erat usurpata, sed nata ? *Semetipsum autem exinanivit, formam servi accipiens* (Philip. ii. 6, 7) : non ergo amittens illam, sed accipiens istam. Eo modo se exinaniens, quo hic minor apparebat quam apud Patrem manebat. Forma quippe servi accessit, non forma Dei recessit : haec est assumpta, non illa consumpta. Propter hanc dicit : *Pater maior me est* ; propter illam vero : *Ego et Pater unum sumus* (Ioan. x. 30).

2. Hoc atttendat Arianus, et attentione sit sanus : ne contentione sit vanus, aut, quod est peius, insanus. Haec est enim forma servi, in qua Dei Filius minor est, non Patre solo, sed etiam Spiritu sancto : neque id tantum, sed etiam se ipso ; quia idem ipse in forma Dei maior est se ipso. Neque enim homo Christus non dicitur Filius Dei, quod etiam sola caro eius in sepulcro meruit appellari. Nam quid aliud confitemur, cum dicimus credere nos in unigenitum Dei Filium, qui sub

leaving, not the heart? True it is that God, the unconfined by space, quitteth the hearts of those whose ways, if not their footsteps, wander from Him, and cometh unto them who set their faith, if not their faces, towards Him, approaching Him in mind instead of body. But that they might understand that it was in respect of His Manhood that He had said: *I go away and come to you,* He further said: *If ye loved Me, ye would surely rejoice because I go unto the Father; for the Father is greater than I.* In that respect then in which the Son is not equal to the Father, He was to go to the Father, from Him to return to judge the quick and the dead; in that in which the Only-Begotten is the equal of the Begetter, He goeth never from the Father, but is in all His fulness with Him everywhere, in virtue of an equal Godhead which no place confines. For, *being in the Form of God,* as the Apostle hath it, *He thought it not usurpation to be equal with God.* For how could that be usurpation which was a natural right, inherited, and not usurped? *He emptied Himself, taking the form of a servant* (Phil. ii. 6, 7), taking the servant's form and yet not thereby losing that of God; emptied Himself in such sort that He displayed Himself on earth in a position inferior to that wherein He was abiding with the Father, for in truth the servant's form was taken, but the Form of God was not forsaken; that was assumed, but this was not consumed; the former enabled Him to say: *The Father is greater than I*; the latter: *I and the Father are One* (Jn. x. 30).

2. Let the Arian attend to this and through attention win his sanity, lest his contention end in vanity, or, what is worse, in insanity. This is that form of a servant in which the Son of God is inferior, not to the Father only, but also to the Holy Spirit; ay, even to Himself; for being in the Form of God, He is greater even than Himself. Think not that the Man Christ is not called the Son of God; His mere flesh in the tomb could claim that name. What else do we confess when we say that we believe in the Only-Begotten Son of

Pontio Pilato crucifixus est et sepultus? Et quid eius nisi caro sepulta est sine anima? Ac per hoc cum credimus in Dei Filium qui sepultus est, profecto Filium Dei dicimus et carnem, quae sola sepulta est. Ipse ergo Christus Filius Dei, aequalis Patri in forma Dei, quia *semetipsum exinanivit*, non formam Dei amittens, sed *formam servi accipiens*, maior est et se ipso : quia maior est forma Dei quae amissa non est, quam servi quae accepta est. Quid itaque mirum vel quid indignum, si secundum hanc formam servi loquens, ait Dei Filius : *Pater maior me est* ; et secundum Dei formam loquens, ait idem ipse Dei Filius : *Ego et Pater unum sumus* ? Unum sunt enim secundum id quod Deus erat Verbum : maior est Pater, secundum id quod Verbum caro factum est. Dicam etiam quod Ariani et Eunomiani negare non possunt, secundum hanc formam servi puer Christus etiam parentibus suis minor erat, quando parvus maioribus, sicut scriptum est, *subditus* erat (Luc. ii. 51). Quid igitur, haeretice, cum Christus Deus sit et homo, loquitur ut homo, et calumniaris Deo ? Ille in se naturam commendat humanam, tu in illo audes deformare divinam ? Infidelis, ingrate, ideone tu minuis eum qui fecit te, quia dicit ille quid factus sit propter te ? Aequalis enim Patri Filius per quem factus est homo, ut minor esset Patre, factus est homo : quod nisi fieret, quid esset homo ?

3. Dicat plane Dominus et magister noster : *Si diligeretis me, gauderetis utique, quia vado ad Patrem ; quia Pater maior me est*. Cum discipulis audiamus verba doctoris, non cum alienis sequamur astutiam deceptoris. Agnoscamus geminam substantiam Christi, divinam scilicet qua aequalis

God, who under Pontius Pilate was crucified and buried?
And what of Him was buried but the flesh without the soul?
Therefore, believing in the Son of God, who was buried, we
cannot but give the name of Son of God even to the flesh
which by itself was buried. Therefore the selfsame Christ,
the Son of God, equal to the Father in the Form of God, is
greater even than Himself; for *He emptied Himself*, not
putting off the Form of God, but *putting on the form of a
servant*; the Form of God, which was not put off, being greater
than the servant's form, which was put on. Where is the
wonder then, where the loss of dignity, if the Son of God says,
speaking in accordance with the servant's form, *The Father is
greater than I*, whereas in speaking in accordance with the
Form of God, the selfsame Son of God declares, *I and the
Father are One*? One they are, because *the Word was God*;
greater is the Father, because *the Word was made flesh*. And
I will say what Arians and Eunomians cannot deny; that, as
touching the form of a servant, the child Christ was less even
than His parents, when as a little one, as it is written, He was
subject to His elders (Lu. ii. 51). How then, thou heretic,
since Christ is God and Man, doth He speak as man, and dost
thou dare blaspheme Him as God? He honoureth man's
nature in Himself, and dost thou dare dishonour God's in
Him? Faithless ingrate, is it for this thou degradest Him
that made thee because He telleth thee what He became for
thee? For He by whom man was made, the Son, the equal
of the Father, was Himself made man, to be inferior to the
Father; and what would have become of man if He had not
become Man?

3. By all means therefore let our Lord and Master say
plainly: *If ye loved Me, ye would surely rejoice because I go
unto the Father; for the Father is greater than I.* With the
disciples let us hear the teacher's words; not with the aliens
be led away by the deceiver's craft. Let us acknowledge the
twofold nature of Christ: the divine, by which He is the

est Patri, humanam qua maior est Pater.   Utrumque autem
simul non duo, sed unus est Christus ; ne sit quaternitas, non
Trinitas Deus.   Sicut enim unus est homo anima rationalis et
caro, sic unus est Christus Deus et homo : ac per hoc Christus
est Deus anima rationalis et caro.   Christum in his omnibus,
Christum in singulis confitemur.   Quis est ergo per quem
factus est mundus ?   Christus Iesus, sed in forma Dei.   Quis
est sub Pontio Pilato crucifixus ?   Christus Iesus, sed in
forma servi.   Item de singulis quibus homo constat.   Quis
non est derelictus in inferno ?   Christus Iesus, sed in anima
sola.   Quis resurrecturus triduo iacuit in sepulcro ?   Christus
Iesus, sed in carne sola.   Dicitur ergo et in his singulis
Christus.   Verum haec omnia non duo, vel tres, sed unus est
Christus.   Ideo ergo dixit : *Si diligeretis me, gauderetis utique,
quia vado ad Patrem* : quia naturae humanae gratulandum
est, eo quod sic assumpta est a Verbo unigenito, ut immortalis
constitueretur in caelo, atque ita fieret terra sublimis, ut
incorruptibilis pulvis sederet ad dexteram Patris.   Hoc enim
modo se iturum dixit ad Patrem.   Nam profecto ad illum ibat
qui cum illo erat.   Sed hoc erat ire ad eum et recedere a
nobis, mutare atque immortale facere quod mortale suscepit
ex nobis, et levare in caelum per quod fuit in terra pro nobis.
Quis non hinc gaudeat, qui sic diligit Christum, ut et suam
naturam iam immortalem gratuletur in Christo, atque id se
speret futurum esse per Christum ?

Father's equal, and the human, by which the Father is greater
than He.   But He is both at once, not two persons but One
Christ; lest we make the Godhead a Quaternity, not a Trinity.
For as the reasonable soul and flesh is one man, so God and
man is One Christ; and therefore Christ is God, reasonable soul and flesh.   Christ we confess in all these aspects,
Christ in each by itself.   Who then made the world?   Christ
Jesus, in the Form of God.   Who was crucified under Pontius
Pilate?   Christ Jesus, in the servant's form.   And so in respect
of each part of man's nature by itself.   Who is He who was
not left in Hell?   Christ Jesus, but in respect of His soul
alone.   Who lay for three days in the tomb, to rise again?
Christ Jesus, but in respect of His flesh alone.   Thus we speak
of each of these elements of human nature by itself as Christ.
Yet all these are not two, or three, but One Christ.   Therefore He said: *If ye loved Me ye would surely rejoice because I
go unto the Father*, because it should be a cause for joy to
human nature that it was so assumed by the Only-Begotten
Word as to be placed immortal in heaven, and that earth
should be raised so high that dust should sit imperishable at
the right hand of the Father.   For in this sense He spake of
going to the Father.   He went indeed to Him who was with
Him all the time; but the going to Him and the leaving us
was simply this, to change and make immortal that mortal
which He took of us, and to raise to heaven that by means of
which He came on earth for us.   Who shall not then rejoice
at this, who so loves Christ, that he sees to his joy his own
nature made immortal now in Christ, and hopes that he
himself too will one day through Christ become immortal?

TRACTATUS LXXIX.

De eo quod ait: *Et nunc dixi vobis prius quam fiat* etc.,
usque ad id: *Surgite, eamus hinc* (xiv. 29—31).

1. Dominus et salvator noster Iesus Christus dixerat
discipulis suis: *Si diligeretis me, gauderetis utique, quia vado
ad Patrem, quia Pater maior me est* (Ioan. xiv. 28). Quod ex
forma servi eum dixisse, non ex forma Dei, in qua aequalis
est Patri, novit fides quae religiosis est mentibus fixa, non
calumniosis et dementibus ficta. Deinde subiunxit: *Et nunc
dixi vobis prius quam fiat, ut cum factum fuerit, credatis.*
Quid est hoc, cum magis homo credere debeat antequam fiat
id quod credendum est? Haec est enim laus fidei, si quod
creditur non videtur. Nam quid magnum est, si creditur
quod videtur, secundum illam eiusdem Domini sententiam,
quando discipulum arguit dicens: *Quia vidisti, credidisti;
beati qui non vident et credunt* (ib. xx. 29)? Et nescio utrum
credere dicendus est quisque quod videt: nam ipsa fides in
epistola quae scribitur ad Hebraeos, ita est definita: *Est
autem fides sperantium*[1] *substantia, convictio rerum quae non
videntur* (Hebr. xi. 1). Quapropter si fides est rerum quae
creduntur, eademque fides earum est quae non videntur:
quid sibi vult quod Dominus ait: *Et nunc dixi vobis prius
quam fiat, ut cum factum fuerit, credatis*? Nonne potius
dicendum fuit: Et nunc dixi vobis prius quam fiat, ut credatis quod cum factum fuerit videatis? Nam et ille cui
dictum est: *Quia vidisti, credidisti*, non hoc credidit quod

* Tres MSS. *sperandorum.*

HOMILY LXXIX.

From the words, *And now I have told you before it come to pass* etc., as far as, *Arise, let us go hence* (xiv. 29—31).

1. Our Lord and Saviour Jesus Christ had said to His disciples: *If ye loved Me, you would surely rejoice because I go unto the Father; for the Father is greater than I* (Jn. xiv. 28). That this is the utterance of the Form of a servant, not of the Form of God wherein He is equal to the Father, faith knows—not faith which is the fruit of mischievous and wild imaginings, but that which has its root struck deep in the religious heart. Then He added: *And now I have told you before it come to pass, that, when it is come to pass, ye may believe.* How is this? If a thing has a claim on our belief, ought we not rather to believe it *before* it come to pass? For this is the glory of faith, that it believes what is not seen. It is but a small thing to believe what we see, as we know from that declaration of the selfsame Lord when He reproved His disciple with the words: *Because thou hast seen, thou hast believed; blessed are they who do not see, and yet believe* (ib. xx. 29). Indeed I know not whether a man can be said to believe what he sees; faith in the Epistle written to the Hebrews is defined as follows: *Now fath is the assurance of them that hope, the proof of things not seen* (Hebr. xi. 1). Wherefore if faith refers to things that are believed, and the same faith to things which are not seen, what mean these words of the Lord: *And now I have told you before it come to pass, that when it is come to pass, ye may believe*? Should He not rather have said, "And now I have told you before it come to pass, that ye may believe after it has come to pass what ye see"? Why, even he to whom it was said: *Because thou hast seen, thou hast believed,* believed not what he saw; he saw one

vidit; sed aliud vidit, aliud credidit: vidit enim hominem, credidit Deum. Cernebat quippe atque tangebat carnem viventem, quam viderat morientem: et credebat Deum in carne ipsa latentem. Credebat ergo mente quod non videbat, per hoc quod sensibus corporis apparebat. Sed etsi dicuntur credi quae videntur, sicut dicit unusquisque oculis suis se credidisse: non tamen ipsa est quae in nobis aedificatur fides, sed ex rebus quae videntur, agitur in nobis ut ea credantur quae non videntur. Quocirca, dilectissimi, unde nunc mihi sermo est, quod Dominus ait: *Et nunc dixi vobis prius quam fiat ut cum factum fuerit, credatis:* illud utique dicit, *cum factum fuerit,* quod eum visuri erant post mortem viventem et ad Patrem ascendentem: quo viso illud fuerant credituri, quod ipse esset Christus Filius Dei vivi, qui potuit hoc facere cum praedixisset, et praedicere antequam faceret: credituri autem hoc non fide nova, sed aucta; aut certe cum mortuus esset defecta, cum resurrexisset refecta. Neque enim eum Dei Filium non et ante credebant: sed cum in illo factum esset quod ante praedixit, fides illa, quae tunc quando illis loquebatur fuit parva, et cum moreretur pene iam nulla, et revixit et crevit.

2. Deinde quid dicit? *Iam non multa loquor vobiscum: venit enim princeps mundi huius:* quis, nisi diabolus? *Et in me non habet quidquam:* nullum scilicet omnino peccatum. Sic enim ostendit non creaturarum, sed peccatorum principem diabolum, quos nunc nomine mundi huius appellat. Et quotiescunque mundi nomen in mali significatione ponitur, non ostendit nisi mundi istius amatores; de quibus alibi scriptum est: *Quicunque voluerit amicus esse saeculi huius, inimicus Dei constituetur* (Iacob. iv. 4). Absit ergo ut sic intelligatur diabolus princeps mundi tamquam gerat universi

thing, believed another; for what he saw was man, what he
believed was God. The flesh that he had seen in death he
saw and touched in life; and he believed that it was God who
was concealed beneath that flesh. That which was manifest to
bodily sense empowered him to believe in heart what he did
not see. But albeit things which are seen are said to be
believed as when a man says he has believed his own eyes,
this is not the faith that is being built up in us; but the
effect on us of things that are seen is to produce faith in the
things that are not seen. Wherefore, my well-beloved, in this
utterance of our Lord on which my sermon is based: *And now
I have told you before it be come to pass, that, when it is come
to pass, ye may believe*, the words, *when it is come to pass*,
mean surely this, that they should see Him after His death,
alive, ascending to the Father; that, seeing this, they should
believe that He was Christ the Son of the living God, who
both had power to do this after He had foretold it, and to
foretell it before He did it; that they should believe this not
by a new, but by a larger faith, a faith which, though decayed
at His death, was of a surety new-made at His resurrection.
Not that they did not even before believe Him to be Son of
God, but that when that came to pass in Him which He had
before foretold, their faith which at the time that He spake to
them was small, and when He died was almost nothing, then
not only revived, but grew.

2. What saith He next? *Hereafter I will not talk much
with you; for the prince of this world cometh* (who but the
devil?) *and hath nothing in Me*; that is, no touch of sin
at all. Hereby He shews the devil to be prince not of created
things as such, but of sinful men, whom He here designates by
the name of *this world*. Whenever the name "world" is used in
a bad sense, it denotes simply lovers of this world; of whom it
is elsewhere written: *Whosoever will be the friend of this world
shall become the enemy of God* (Jas. iv. 4). God forbid that
we should understand the devil to be prince of the world in

mundi, id est, caeli et terrae atque omnium quae in eis sunt, principatum : de quali mundo dictum est, cum de Christo Verbo sermo esset : *Et mundus per eum factus est* (Ioan. i. 10). Universus itaque mundus a summis caelis usque ad infimam terram creatori est subditus, non desertori ; redemptori, non interemptori ; liberatori, non captivatori; doctori, non deceptori. Quemadmodum autem sit intelligendus princeps mundi diabolus, evidentius aperuit Paulus apostolus, qui cum dixisset : *Non est nobis colluctatio adversus carnem et sanguinem*, id est, adversus homines ; subiecit atque ait : *sed adversus principes et potestates et rectores mundi tenebrarum harum* (Ephes. vi. 12). Sequenti enim verbo exposuit quid dixisset *mundi*, cum subiecit, *tenebrarum harum* : ne quisquam mundi nomine intelligeret universam creaturam, cuius nullo modo sunt rectores angeli desertores. *Tenebrarum*, inquit, *harum*, id est, mundi istius amatorum : ex quibus tamen electi sunt, non per suum meritum, sed per Dei gratiam, quibus dicit : *Fuistis enim aliquando tenebrae, nunc autem lux in Domino* (ib. v. 8). Omnes enim fuerunt sub rectoribus tenebrarum harum, id est, hominum impiorum, tamquam tenebrae sub tenebris : sed *gratias Deo, qui eruit nos*, sicut dicit idem Apostolus, *de potestate tenebrarum, et transtulit in regnum Filii caritatis suae* (Col. i. 13) : in quo princeps huius mundi, hoc est tenebrarum harum, non habebat quidquam : quia neque cum peccato Deus venerat, nec eius carnem de peccati propagine virgo pepererat. Et tamquam ei diceretur : Cur ergo moreris, si non habes peccatum, cui debeatur mortis supplicium ? continuo subiecit : *Sed ut cognoscat mundus, quia diligo Patrem, et sicut mandatum dedit mihi Pater, sic facio ; surgite, eamus hinc* (Ioan. xiv. 31). Discumbens enim discumbentibus loquebatur. *Eamus* autem dixit, quo, nisi ad illum locum unde fuerat tradendus ad mortem, qui nullum

the sense of bearing rule over the whole world, i.e. heaven and earth and all that therein is, of which world it was said in a passage treating of Christ the Word, *And the world was made by Him* (Jn. i. 10). No, the whole world from highest heaven to the depths of earth is subject to the Creator, not to the renegade; to the restorer, not to the destroyer; to the deliverer, not to the enslaver; to the teacher, not to the deceiver. But the sense in which we are to understand the devil to be prince of the world is more clearly declared by the Apostle Paul, when after saying: *We wrestle not against flesh and blood*, i.e. against men, he goes on to say, *but against princes and powers and rulers of the world of this darkness* (Eph. vi. 12). He has explained what he meant by *world* by the further words, *of this darkness*; that none should understand world to mean the whole creation, of which the rebel angels are in no way rulers. *Of this darkness*, i.e. of the lovers of this world, from the number of whom however they are chosen, not for their own merit but by the grace of God, to whom he says: *For ye were sometime darkness, but now light in the Lord* (ib. v. 8). They all were under the rulers of this darkness, i.e. of the ungodly—darkness as it were under darkness—but *thanks be to God*, as saith the same Apostle, *who hath delivered us from the power of darkness, and hath translated us into the kingdom of the Son of His love* (Col. i. 13). In Him the prince of this world, i.e. of this darkness, had nothing; for God came not with sin into the world, nor did the virgin bring to birth His flesh of the stock of sin. And as though it were said to Him, Why then diest Thou, if Thou hast not sin to merit the punishment of death? He forthwith added: *But that the world may know that I love the Father, and as the Father gave Me commandment, even so do I; arise, let us go hence* (Jn. xiv. 31). They were sitting at meat together, He and they, while He spake these words. Then *let us go*, He said. Whither, but to that place whence He that had done nothing worthy of death was to be delivered up to death?

habebat meritum mortis ? Sed habebat ut moreretur mandatum Patris, tamquam ille de quo praedictum erat : *Quae
non rapui, tunc exsolvebam* (Psal. lxviii. 5) : mortem sine debito
soluturus, et nos a morte debita redempturus. Rapuerat
autem Adam peccatum, quando manum in arborem prae-
sumptione deceptus extendit, ut incommunicabile nomen
inconcessae divinitatis invaderet, quam Filio Dei natura con-
tulerat, non rapina.

Ay, but He had His Father's commandment that He should die, as the very One of whom it had been prophesied, *I paid the things I never took* (Ps. lxix. 4); paying the debt of death which was not due from Him, redeeming us from the death which was our due. But Adam had taken something, viz. sin, when in blind wilfulness he put his hand forth to the tree, meaning to seize by force the incommunicable name of deity, of deity which had not been conveyed to him, but was the Son of God's, not by usurpation, but by natural right.

HINTS ON GRAMMAR.

Students not conversant with the language of St Augustine's age should consult Rönsch, *Itala und Vulgata* (1875), Paucker, *De Latinitate B. Hieronymi* (1880), Goelzer, *Latinité de St Jérôme* (1884), Regnier, *Latinité des sermons de St Augustin* (1886), E. W. Watson, *Style of St Cyprian (Studia Biblica* v.). There is of course strictly speaking no Augustinian Latin. The speech is the speech of the period, and divergences from it on the part of Augustine are deliberately rhetorical. All that is here attempted is to furnish (*a*) a list of the less familiar usages and (*b*) a vocabulary of unclassical words appearing in these homilies, whether they occur in Augustine's own words or in his Biblical quotations.

I. USE OF VERB.

1. Mood.

(A) Indicative for Subjunctive.

(*a*) In indirect questions: et quo ego *vado* scitis lxvii. 4 *etc.*—nescimus quo *vadis* lxix. 1.

(*b*) After cum: cum eorum...corda *mundantur* lxix. 1—cum idem populus *est* in Deo lxix. 1.

(B) Subjunctive for Indicative.
eo quod male *petatis* lxxiii. 1.

(C) Infinitive.

(*a*) For ut with the subjunctive: cum...restaret *nosse* lxix. 2—restat *inquirere* lxxii. 3 (contrast restat ergo ut intelligamus lxxiv. 2 and cp. restabat verba *referre*, Ovid *Met.* i. 700).

(*b*) Of purpose after a verb of motion: vado *parare* lxvii. 2 *etc.*—vadis parare lxvii. 4.

2. TENSE.

The ordinary sequence is often disregarded : thus we find

(A) **Present** where **Future** might be expected.

Venio et accipiam lxvii. 4 *etc.*

(B) **Pluperfect** where **Imperfect** might be expected.

ut quod in spe *fueratis,* etiam in re esse possitis lxviii. 2—qui (*sc.* Spiritus) quantum habendus *fuerat* nondum habebant lxxiv. 2— habebant occulte, accepturi *fuerant* manifeste ib.—ita eum (*sc.* Spiritum) Dominus daturus *fuerat* lxxv. 1—quo viso illud *fuerant* credituri lxxix. 1 —quo, nisi ad illum locum unde *fuerat* tradendus ad mortem lxxix. 2.

3. GERUND AND GERUNDIVE.

(A) **Ablative of Gerund** for **Present Participle.**

eos haec scire convicerat *addendo* atque *dicendo* lxx. 2—*errando* in diversâ istis lxxi. 2—loquebatur *dicendo* lxxiii. 2—neque enim mentitus est *dicendo* lxxvi. 5 (cp. ita miserrimus fui *fugitando,* Ter. *Eun.* v. 28).

(B) **Gerundive** for **Future Participle Passive.**

dandus erat...amplius lxxiv. 2—fuerat *tradendus* lxxix. 2.

II. USE OF CONJUNCTIONS.

Quod, quia with the finite verb for the accusative and infinitive.

> *The use of these conjunctions, which thus comes to correspond generally with that of ὅτι, might be attributed to Greek influence, but* **scio quod** *occurs in early Latin, and there is evidence that the construction belonged to the popular language.*

(*a*) quod: cognovimus *quod sciebant* viam lxix. 2—scio *quod* te *exinanisti* lxix. 3—si dicamus *quod...sciebant* lxx. 2—ne quisquam putaret *quod...daturus fuerat* lxxv. 1—non videbat *quod...*Verbum *latebat* lxxv. 2 —verum est...quod...*fuerat subtracturus* lxxvi. 3—credimus *quod* invicem *diligamus* lxxvii. 4.

(*b*) quia: dixissem...*quia vado* lxvii. 2 *etc.*—significas *quia...*vivere *debet* iustus lxviii. 3—credis *quia...*Pater in me *est* lxx. 3—sed dixeramus...*quia* maius *fuit* lxxii. 1—*quia* vero et nos...in illo *sumus* ostendit lxxv. 4—cognoscemus *quia* ipse in Patre (*est*) ib.—cum credimus *quia est* lxxvii. 3—audistis *quia* ego *dixi* lxxviii. 1—sed ut cognoscat mundus *quia diligo* Patrem lxxix. 2.

III. USE OF ADVERBS.

(A) Adverbs of Place Used Metaphorically.

(*a*) ubi: cum dixisset...*ubi* satis ostendit lxviii. 1—dixerat enim... *ubi* intelleximus lxix. 1—hoc promissum *ubi* ait lxxiii. 2—sponsi filios nos appellat *ubi* dicit lxxv. 1 (cp. cum multa colligeres et ex legibus et ex senatus consultis, *ubi*, si verba, non rem sequeremur, confici nihil posset, Cic. *de Or.* i. 57. 243).

(*b*) hinc: non parva *hinc* exoritur quaestio lxxii. 3—*hinc* est quod etiam sponsi filios nos appellat lxxv. 1—*hinc* fortasse intelligendum est esse dictum lxxv. 2—*hinc* ergo turbari poterat cor lxxviii. 1 (cp. *hinc* illae lacrimae, Ter. *Andr.* 126).

(*c*) unde: *unde* audire debuerunt lxvii. 2—*unde* dicit idem apostolus lxviii. 2—*unde* illa vox est lxx. 1—*unde* profecto qui non custodit, non diligit lxxii. 2—si hoc ab illo petitur *unde* homo laedatur lxxiii. 1—*unde* tunc expedit potius lxxiii. 3—*unde* et monet apostolus lxxiv. 3—*unde* intelleximus lxxvii. 1—*unde* nunc mihi sermo est lxxix. 1 (cp. *unde* tu me ex iure manum consertum vocasti, inde ibi ego te revoco, Cic. *Mur.* 12 where unde, inde=qua (ea) de re).

(B) Non.

(*a*) for ne: *non* turbetur cor vestrum lxvii. 1 *etc.*—*non* miremur, non paveamus lxxvi. 5.

(*b*)=No !—*non* utique, quia ipse...habet vitam lxx. 1.

(C) Utique.

Expressing strong affirmation = *val*: quo *utique* denario vita signi-ficatur lxvii. 2—coarctata *utique* non clarebunt lxvii. 4—tunc *utique* quando eos vocavit lxviii. 1—et *utique* non aliud est vita lxx. 1—non *utique*, quia ipse exsistendo habet vitam ib.—non ob aliud nisi quod ipsum *utique* scirent lxx. 2—per me *utique* et illum lxx. 2—*utique* enim quia nemo...venit ib.—non *utique* ut ipse sit Pater ib.—qui ergo non vivet non *utique* credit lxxii. 2—non *utique* sine nobis ib.—quod *utique* in illo...Christus operatur lxxii. 3—et *utique* minus est ib.—nos...qui *utique* non...accipimus lxxiii. 2—*utique* Christus Iesus lxxiii. 3—non *utique* nos salvos faciet ib.—carnis *utique* resurgentis lxxv. 3—intus *utique* tamquam Deus in templo suo lxxvi. 4—non *utique* suum, sed Patris est verbum lxxvi. 5—*utique* praesentia corporali lxxvii. 1—non eos *utique* dicimus simul lxxvii. 2—illud *utique* dicit lxxix. 1.

IV. USE OF PREPOSITIONS.

(A) Ad.

(a) of destination : deputatur fides ejus *ad* iustitiam lxxii. 2.

(b) =in reference to: *ad* nos ipsos turbati sumus lxx. 1—*ad* me ipsum turbata est anima (πρὸς ἐμαυτόν) ib.—quod si *ad* te multum est lxx. 3— sed multum est *ad* nos lxxiv. 1 (cp. nil igitur mors est *ad* nos, Lucr. iii. 830).

(c) of time : Filium autem...*ad* modicum vident lxxvi. 4 (cp. et nos faciamus *ad* annum Pastorum dominae grandia liba Pali, Ovid *Fast.* iv. 775).

(B) De.

(a) for in with the accusative : *de* praesenti...*de* futuro lxxv. 3—*de* cetero lxxvi. 3 (cp. the classical *de* nocte, *de* die, *de* mense).

(b) of the source from which: intelligamus *de* verbis Domini posterioribus priora lxix. 1—Pater...Deus non est .*de* aliquo, Filius autem Deus...*de* Patre Deo lxxi. 1—Deus...*de* Deo...lumen *de* lumine ib.

(C) In.

(a) with accusative after credere : credite *in* Deum lxvii. 1 (see note *ad loc.*) etc.—credendo *in* eum lxix. 1—credere *in*...Dei Filium lxxviii. 2.

(b) with ablative (1) of instrument : non *in* eo (ἐν τούτῳ) discernens lxvii. 2; (2) of manner : *in* nomine meo lxxiii. 1—*in* nomine Salvatoris lxxiii. 3.

(D) Per.

With hoc, id=itaque or ideo quod: ac *per* hoc et ipse per se ipsum...ad se ipsum (venit) lxix. 2—ergo et ibat *per* id quod homo erat et manebat *per* id quod Deus erat...ibat *per* id quod uno loco erat, manebat *per* id quod ubique erat lxxviii. 1—ac *per* hoc Christus est Deus lxxviii. 3.

V. USE OF PRONOUNS.

(A) Aliquis for alius.

aliquae mansiones in regno...*aliquae* extra regnum lxvii. 3—*aliqui* eorum sciebant, *aliqui* nesciebant lxx. 2.

(B) Ipse.

(a) for idem : mansiones...non aliae sed *ipsae* lxvii. 1—non utique ut *ipse* sit Pater qui Filius lxx. 2—iste *ipse* Iohannes (=hic idem) lxxvi. 3.

(b) for ille (emphatic): quia sciebant *ipsum* qui est via lxix. 2—et
nos quo imus nisi ad *ipsum* ib.—*ipse* igitur per se ipsum ib. and throughout the section—ad veritatem, quod est *ipse*, remeavit lxix. 3—*ipsum*
sciebant lxx. 1 and throughout the section—quod tanto tempore cum
ipsis erat lxx. 2—quod *ipsum* utique scirent ib.—ipse est enim via ib.—
ipso docente qui non recedit a nobis lxxi. 1—alius...Pater, alius *ipse*
lxxi. 2—non *ipsis* tanquam ex se ipsis lxxi. 3—illud per se, hoc per
ipsos, sed tamen utrumque *ipse* ib.—*ipse* quippe sine *ipsis*...fecit lxxii. 1
—*ipse* fieri dignatus est ib.—quid...illi sine *ipso* ib.—non faciet *ipse*...
faciet et *ipse* ib.—non...*ipsos* tantum significans lxxii. 2—Spiritus...in-
sufflatus ab *ipso*...ab *ipso* missus lxxiv. 2—quia vivit *ipse*, vivemus et nos
lxxv. 3—*ipse* in Patre et nos in *ipso* et *ipse* in nobis lxxv. 4—quod et
nunc inchoatum est iam per *ipsum*, ut sit in nobis, et nos in *ipso* ib.
—*ipse* est...qui diligit me lxxv. 5—simus cum *ipsis* lxxvi. 1—quantum
aperire *ipse* dignatur lxxvi. 3—nec *ipsum* in forma Dei lxxvi. 4—cum *ipsi*
non possint esse non simul lxxvii. 3—pax ergo *ipse* nobis est lxxvii. 3.

(C) Iste for hic.

istae mansiones lxxviii. 3—dicit *iste* lxix. 1—*isti* sciebant ib.—in *isto*
sermone lxix. 2—*ista*...vultis exponi ib.—facile *ista* quaestio solvitur
lxx. 2—illum cujus est *iste* similis lxx. 3—*ista* maiora lxxi. 3—quando
ista dicebat ib.—*ista* tractanda sunt...sermo *iste* ib.—sermo *iste* lxxii. 3—
multa sunt...in *istis*...verbis lxxiv. 1—sermo *iste* lxxiv. 2—*iste* ipse
Iohannes lxxvi. 3—sequitur *ista* (lectio) lxxvii. 1—pax vero *ista* lxxvii. 4
—*ista* Domini verba ib.—*istam* pacem ib.—non...amittens illam, sed accipiens *istam* (*sc.* formam) lxxviii. 1—mundi *istius* amatorem lxxix. 2.

(D) Quicunque for quilibet.

non...nos salvos faciet *quicunque* rex lxxiii. 3.

VI. USE OF SUBSTANTIVES.

Cases.

(A) Genitive of comparison.

maiora *horum* (μείζονα τούτων) lxxi. 3 *etc.*—omnium operum Christi
maiora lxxii. 3.

(B) Dative.

(a) Of local relation: fides *mentibus* fixa lxxix. 1 (cp. clipeum *posti-
bus* adversis figo, Virg. *Aen.* iii. 286).

cum *regno* venerit regnum lxviii. 2 (cp. it clamor *caelo*, Virg. *Aen.* v.
451).

(b) Of the person interested: contemptibilis *ei*...amabilis *eis* lxxii. 1—
quod est nomen eius *fidelibus* eius lxxiii. 3—*impiis* damnator...*fidelibus*
salvator ib.—mortui sumus *illi* quando viximus *nobis* lxxv. 3—*mundo*...
contemptibilis...terribilis lxxvi. 4.

(c) After loqui=dicere (cp. extension of λαλεῖν=λέγειν) : si autem
loquor *vobis* lxix. 4—solemus...loqui *eis* lxx. 2—verba quae ego loquor
vobis lxxi. 1—locutus *audientibus* lxxii. 1—quando *illis* loquebatur
lxxix. 1—*discumbentibus* loquebatur lxxix. 2.

(d) After calumniari : calumniaris *Deo* lxxviii. 2.

(C) Accusative.

(a) Of persons after commemorare : commemorabit *vos* omnia
lxxvii. 2.

(b) After credere : credidit *Deum* lxxix. 1 (cp. lxvii. 1 note).

(D) Ablative of duration of time.

tanto tempore vobiscum sum lxx. 2 *etc.*

VII. USE OF ADJECTIVES AND PARTICIPLES.

As Nouns.

*The vocabulary of modern languages descended from Latin
consists largely of words which originally denoted the quality
of an object and have come to denote the object itself.*

adoptatus lxii. 1—Ariani lxxi. 2 *etc.*—carissimi *passim*—ceterum
lxxvi. 3 (see also under adverbial expressions)—debitum lxvii. 4—
dilectissimi *passim*—Eunomiani lxxviii. 2—fideles lxxii. 3 ; lxxiii. 2, 3
etc.—haeretici lxxi. 2—infernum lxxviii. 3—innocentes lxvii. 3—iustus
lxviii. 2 ; lxxii. 2 *etc.*—impius lxxii. 2 ; lxxvi. 2 *etc.*—mendaces lxix. 3—
modicum lxxv. 2 ; lxxvi. 3—Patripassiani lxxi. 2 *etc.*—praedestinati
lxxii. 3—peccatum *passim*—Sabelliani lxxi. 2 *etc.*—sperantes lxxiii. 1.

VOCABULARY OF NEW WORDS.

An asterisk denotes classical words used in a new sense.

(A) Substantives.

(a) In -**mentum** : indumentum lxxv. 2—aeramentum lxxvi. 2—
*sacramentum lxxii. 3, lxxvi. 2.

(b) In -**ura** : creatura lxvii. 3, lxxiii. 1, lxxix. 2.

(c) In -**ntia**: concupiscentia lxxiii. 1—distantia lxx. 3—inoboedientia
lxxiii. 1—praesentia lxviii. 2, lxxvii. 1—*sapientia lxxiii. 1—substantia
lxxvi. 2, lxxviii. 3—*scientia lxxiv. 3—temperantia lxxiv. 3.

(d) In -**tas** : *caritas lxvii. 2 etc.—quaternitas lxxviii. 3—Trinitas
lxxiv. 1 etc.—unitas lxvii. 2 etc.

(e) In -**tor**: captivator lxxix. 2—*creator lxxix. 2—damnator lxxiii. 3—
deceptor lxxviii. 3, lxxix. 2—dilector lxxiv. 4, lxxvi. 4—interemptor
lxxix. 2—mansor lxviii. 2—mediator lxxiv. 3—peccator lxxix. 2—*re-
demptor lxxix. 2—salvator lxxiii. 3.

(f) In -**do** : plenitudo lxxiv. 3.

(g) In -**io**: colluctatio lxxix. 2—constitutio lxviii. 1—consummatio
ib.—*convictio lxxix. 1—defectio lxxii. 1—dignatio lxxii. 1—dilatio
lxxii. 3—inhabitatio lxix. 2—impertitio lxxiv. 2—iustificatio lxxii. 3 etc.
—manifestatio lxxiv. 2, lxxvi. 2—mansio lxvii. 3 etc.—*offensio lxxiii. 1
—*oratio lxxiii. 3, 4—praedestinatio lxviii. 1 etc.—*praesumptio lxxix. 2
—resurrectio lxvii. 2 etc.—*tentatio lxvii. 2, lxxiii. 4.

(h) In -**us** : *mundus passim—*salus lxxii. 3—*spiritus passim.

(i) In -**um** : Verbum (sc. Dei) passim.

(j) In -**o**: *caro passim—*sermo (sc. Dei) passim.

(k) **Foreign words** : angelus lxxvi. 2, 3—apostolus passim—baptis-
mum lxvii. 3—Christus passim—diabolus lxxix. 2—evangelista lxxvi. 3—
evangelium lxviii. 3, lxxiv. 1 etc.—manna lxxiii. 1—orphanus lxxv. 1—
Paracletus lxxiv. 1, 4—petra lxxii. 2—psalmus lxxvi. 2—scandalum
lxviii. 2—zizania ib.

110 VOCABULARY OF NEW WORDS.

(B) Adjectives.

(a) In -alis: carnalis lxvii. 3, lxix. 3—consubstantialis lxxiv. 1—corporalis lxxvii. 1—rationalis lxxviii. 3.

(b) In -bilis: contemptibilis lxxii. 1, lxxvi. 4—culpabilis lxxiii. 1—incommunicabilis lxxix. 2—incorruptibilis lxxviii. 3—invisibilis lxxiv. 4 etc.—visibilis lxxvii. 1 etc.

(c) In -anus: Arianus passim—Eunomianus lxxviii. 2 etc.—mundanus lxxiv. 4—Patripassianus lxx. 2 etc.—Sabellianus lxx. 2 etc.

(d) In -eus, -ius: carneus lxxv. 2—transitorius lxxvi. 4.

(e) Compounded with modus: omnimodus lxx. 2.

(f) Greek words: apostolicus lxxiv. 1 etc.—canonicus lxxvi. 1 etc.—catholicus lxvii. 3 etc.—evangelicus lxviii. 3 etc.—haereticus lxxi. 2 etc.—propheticus lxxiv. 3.

(g) Miscellaneous: coaeternus lxxiv. 1—dominicus lxxiii. 4—*infidelis lxxviii. 2—*inordinatus lxviii. 1—unigenitus lxxii. 1, lxxviii. 2 etc.

(C) Adverbs.

(a) In -ter: immutabiliter lxx. 1—indifferenter lxxvi. 5—inseparabiliter lxx. 1, lxxv. 5, lxxvii. 2—invisibiliter lxxiv. 4, 5—pluraliter lxx. 3, lxxvi. 5—praetereunter lxxi. 3—spiritaliter lxix. 2—veraciter lxxiv. 1—visibiliter lxxiv. 5.

(b) Adverbial expressions: amodo (ἀπ’ ἄρτι) lxx. 2—de cetero lxxvi. 3—putamus, putatis (= tandem) lxviii. 1, 2; lxix. 2—si quo minus (εἰ δὲ μή) lxvii. 1 etc. (cp. hoc si minus verbis, re cogitur confiteri Cic. Fat. 10).

(D) Verbs.

abesse (absit = μὴ γένοιτο) lxvii. 3; lxxv. 5—adimplere lxxi. 2—*aedificare (metaphorical) lxxi. 1—*apparere lxxviii. 1; lxxix. 1—baptizare lxvii. 3 etc.-beatificare lxxvi. 4—*cognoscere lxix. 2—confortare lxxiv. 3—cooperari lxxii. 3—crucifigere lxxviii. 2, 3—*debere (as auxiliary) lxviii. 3—*deputare lxxii. 2—evangelizare lxxi. 3; lxxiv. 3—exinanire lxvii. 1; lxxviii. 2—exorbitare lxxi. 2—*facere lxxii. 3; lxxvi. 3—glorificare lxxi. 3; lxxiii. 4—*habere (opus) lxviii. 3—*insinuare lxxvii. 2—insufflare lxxiv. 2—ieiunare lxxv. 1—*iustificare lxxii. 2—manducare lxxiii. 1—*mittere lxxiv. 2—*mundare (metaphorical) lxviii. 3—pluere (passive) lxxiii. 1—praedestinare lxviii. 1 etc.—*praedicare lxxii. 1—praescire lxxii. 3—*recolere lxxvi. 4; lxxvii. 2—*redimere lxxix. 2—*scire lxix. 1, 2; lxx. 2; lxxiv. 1—similare lxxii. 2—subaudire lxxvii. 4—*usurpare lxxviii. 1—*valere (δύνασθαι) lxx. 2—vivificare lxxi. 2.

NOTES.

LXVII.

Page 2.

Tractatus] The regular word for an address or sermon (Tertullian, Cyprian, Ambrose, Hilary), and the equivalent of ὁμιλία as Aug. himself tells us: *tractatus populares quos ὁμιλίας Graeci vocant* (*Ep.* ccxxiv.). He gives however identically the same definition of *sermo = λόγος* in *Enarr. in Ps.* cviii. Cp. below § 4 *hodierno sermoni*.

The special application of *tractare, tractatus*, etc. to the 'treatment' of Scripture in church, i.e. preaching, is derived from the Vulg. of 2 Tim. ii. 15 : *recte tractantem* (ὀρθοτομοῦντα) *verbum veritatis.*

Tractatus is however sometimes applied to expositions of Scripture which are not cast in sermon form, and many ὁμιλίαι or *tractatus* (e.g. those of Origen) are more like lectures than sermons in the modern sense.

§ 1.

Erigenda...maior intentio] The words would have especial force if there were evidence to shew that the African rite had some expression such as *attendamus* by way of equivalent to the Greek deacon's exclamation πρόσχωμεν before the Gospel. The omission indeed would be quite exceptional; for the Roman rite at present and for a long time past is certainly singular in not containing some such feature, though a survival of it is to be found in the *state cum silentio audientes intente* quoted by Duchesne, *Origines du culte chrétien*, p. 162. Cp. Intr. § 2 (*a*).

quae modo...sonuerunt] For the place of the sermon in public worship see Intr. § 2 (*a*).

credite] Vulg. has *creditis in Deum*, which is reproduced in a few MSS. of our homilies. The Greek πιστεύετε of course admits of either rendering. Both A.V. and R.V. translate by the indicative, but R.V. margin offers the imperative as alternative.

in Deum] For Aug.'s distinction between *credere illi = credere vera esse quae loquitur ; credere illum = credere quia* (that) *ipse est Deus ;* and *credere in illum = diligere eum*, see Pearson, *On the Creed*, Art. 1.

Belief in God is an act of love as well as an act of faith.

ne mortem...timerent] *mortem* refers in the first instance to Christ. The fear arising from the thought of this is removed by the affirmation of His immortal Godhead. But they had also the prospect of their own death to terrify them, and thus, *et sibi metuebant*, § 2.

rapina] See Lightfoot, *On Philippians* ii. 6.

rapina (ἁρπαγμός) may denote either the act of robbery, or the result of robbery (something attained or to be attained thereby). The ambiguity of the Latin is preserved in the English 'usurpation.'

formam Dei...formam servi] See Lightfoot as above.

§ 2.

unde] See Hints on Grammar, p. 105.

Page 4.

ab illo perituri] *illo* must refer to Christ. It is true that *perire ab aliquo* is often used as passive of *occido*='to be slain by' (e.g. *discipulo perii solus ab ipse meo*, Ovid), but the context forbids this sense here. The phrase, though a curious one, is highly expressive of a process of total separation and decay; a rotten branch might almost be described as 'perishing from its tree.'

quia vado parare] See Hints on Grammar, p. 104.

denarius] By the 'penny' Augustine understands eternal life, which is bestowed equally on all heirs of the kingdom, and he finds in this equality of reward the main lesson of the parable. There are however other possible interpretations, for which see Trench, *On the Parables*, pp. 153 ff. (2nd ed.); Maurice, *Unity of the New Testament*, p. 93; Winterbotham, *The kingdom of heaven here and hereafter*, p. 125.

in eo] See Hints on Grammar, p. 106.

amplius...vivit] = "more fully," rather than "longer," as in the translation.

sed multae mansiones etc.] Although there is equality of reward, there is diversity of rank in the kingdom. This view, which goes back to Origen (cp. Bigg, *Christian Platonists*, p. 233), was widely current in the middle ages, cp.

> Ma tutti fanno bello il primo giro,
> E differentemente han dolce vita.
>
> Dante, *Paradiso* iv. 35, 36.

gloria] See Table of Readings.

nullus separatur a regno] For the form of expression, cp.

> Nella corte del ciel ond' io rivegno,
> Si trovan molte gioie care e belle
> Tanto che *non si posson trar del regno*.
>
> Dante, *Paradiso* x. 72.

in regno] *regnum*=the Messianic kingdom, i.e. the perfect order of things which already exists in heaven, to which the baptized, i.e. the members of the church on earth, look to be admitted. It is too much to say that Aug. regards the 'church,' and the 'kingdom,' as interchangeable terms, notwithstanding the assertion *ecclesia iam nunc est regnum (de Civ.* xx. 9) which he is the first of extant Christian writers to make; even there he does not mean that the church is actually the kingdom, but rather that it is so potentially, the full realization being reserved until the end of all things. The church visible and the church invisible were to his mind identical but not coextensive. For a full discussion of his opinion, see Reuter, *Augustinische Studien*, pp. 106 ff.

caritas] The Latin translators of the Bible were confronted by the same difficulty with regard to *amor* as the Greek translators and writers with regard to ἔρως. Both words were rendered unfit as descriptions of higher love, whether of God or man, by degrading associations, and so the Greeks employed ἀγάπη (of which there is no authenticated instance outside the Bible, except one passage in Philo (*Deus immut.* 14), who may well have borrowed it from the LXX.), and the Latins took *caritas* (after trying *agape*; cp. Cypr. *Test.* iii. 3). Christian feeling in England has been sufficient to enable the simple word 'love' to be used of all kinds of affection. Its use to express the lower does not disable it for the expression of the higher.

The student should consult Bp Lightfoot's note on St Ignatius's famous phrase ὁ ἐμὸς ἔρως ἐσταύρωται (Rom. vii.).

per caritatem fiat......unitas caritatis] Cp. *Nullo modo fit minor accedente socio possessio bonitatis quam tanto latius, quanto concordius possidet individua sociorum caritas.* Aug. *de Civ. Dei* xv. 15.

This noble application of St Paul's principle of unity (cp. Rom. xii. 4; 1 Cor. xii. 12 ff.; Eph. iv. 15; Col. i. 8) is the probable source of at least one other passage in Dante:

> Chè per quanti si dice più lì nostro,
> Tanto possiede più di ben ciascuno
> E più di caritate arde in quel chiostro.
>
> *Purgatorio* xv. 55—57.

Cp. also *Paradiso* iii. 65 ff.

§ 3.

a corde christiano] Abl. of agent, not of motion from. They are to be excommunicated.

qui putant, etc.] i.e. the Pelagians (see Intr. § 1), who used this text to parry Jn. iii. 5. They admitted that, in accordance with Jn.

iii. 5, the kingdom could only be reached through holy baptism, but they drew a distinction between the kingdom and life eternal, maintaining on the strength of Jn. xiv. 2 that there is room in heaven, albeit outside the kingdom, for those who have done no sin, but die unbaptized. Augustine in reply presents them with the following dilemma. The Father's house, in which the mansions are, must lie, on the Pelagians' own shewing, either (a) entirely outside, or (b) partly within, partly outside the kingdom. Both ideas are equally untenable.

Augustine is here concerned with refuting Pelagius, and does not directly raise the question of the salvability of unbaptized infants, which his inexorable logic—the premises being original sin and Jn. iii. 5— forced him elsewhere to answer in the negative. Unbaptized, innocent children could not, according to him, enter heaven, nor escape punishment for birth-sin, which however would be the lightest conceivable (*Ep.* ccxv. 1). It is hardly necessary to remark that we are not bound by his conclusions.

Page 6.

sine illo in regnum caelorum intrare non poterunt] Exceptions to this rule admitted by Augustine are: (1) martyrs, baptized in blood; (2) the penitent thief. Cp. *de Baptismo* iv. 22.

catholica fides] The phrase was used before Augustine by Hilary of Poitiers in A.D. 360 (*de Synodis*, 7, 8, 45).

Petri et Pauli] For Peter and Paul as representatives of saints and apostles see Origen, *de Oratione* 14 (Lommatsch, vol. xvii. p. 146).

absit ut...velint habitare vobiscum] i.e. remain in communion with you while still retaining their folly, or in other words, should object to be excommunicated if they will not recant. For *absit* see Hints on Grammar, p. 110.

Page 8. § 4.

sermoni] See note on *tractatus*, § 1.

LXVIII.
§ 1.

si quo minus] See Hints on Grammar, p. 110.

dixissem vobis quia...]=I would have told you that... The Gk. ὅτι is patient of this rendering, but the next verse (3) makes it improbable, as it contains Christ's definite announcement of departure and preparation. Aug. gets over the difficulty, as we shall see, by postulating a twofold preparation, (a) of the dwellings, and (b) of the inmates.

parare...praeparare] The difference between the verbs *parare* = ἐτοι-μάζειν = to prepare, and *praeparare* = προετοιμάζειν = to prepare beforehand, i.e. to decree or appoint (cp. ἃ προητοίμασεν εἰς δόξαν, Vg. *quae praeparavit in gloriam*, Rom. ix. 23) may be rendered by the English 'prepare' and 'provide.'

PAGE 10.

quomodo putamus] See Hints on Grammar, p. 110.

fecit quae futura sunt] See Table of Readings.

si ipse non fecerit] Perhaps rather 'He shall have made,' than 'He shall make,' as in the translation.

praedestinando] See Intr. § 1, and Mozley, *Aug. Theory of Predestination*. The vocation is to active service, i.e. to the execution of the purpose of predestination. The preparation of the mansions answers to the former, their provision to the latter idea.

PAGE 12. § 2.

domum Dei...templum Dei] Christians are regarded as the temple of God (*a*) as a society (Eph. ii. 21; 1 Pet. ii. 5; Ignatius *Eph.* ix.); and (*b*) as individuals (1 Cor. vi 19; Ignatius *Phil.* vii.).

hoc est etiam regnum Dei, etc.] Augustine gives the same explanation again in *de Trin.* i. 8, understanding by *regnum* a concrete kingdom = *ecclesia* (see above on lxvii. 2), the constituent members of which, the *communio sanctorum*, may be described by synecdoche as 'the kingdom.' But there is no doubt that St Paul in 1 Cor. xv. 23, 24, 28 uses βασιλεία in the sense of dominion or rule (cp. Acts i. 6; Hebr. i. 8), and is referring to what Pearson calls Christ's 'economical' kingdom, which ceases when it has gained its end of subduing all hostile powers in heaven and earth. See Pearson, *On the Creed*, p. 272, and Liddon, *Divinity of our Lord*, pp. 230 ff.

tradiderit contemplando etiam Patri suo] The second *tradiderit* repeats the first, picking up the thread after the parenthesis, *id est quos redemit sanguine suo*, which explains *regnum*. *contemplando* is dative of the purpose and *Patri suo* the direct object of the action, attracted as is usual into the case of the gerundive.

permixta zizania] The parable of the tares was largely used by Augustine in his controversy with the Donatists. See Intr. § 1, and cp. Trench, *On the Parables*, Par. II.

iam regnum vocatur] The church is the kingdom nominally and potentially, the perfect realization of its destiny being reserved for the end described in the preceding passage. See note on *regnum*, lxvii. 2.

116   NOTES.

Page 14. § 3.

iustus ex fide] Note the different treatment which the original passage receives at the hands of two Christian teachers. St Paul developing and expanding the thought of Habakkuk ii. 14 (see Kirkpatrick, *Doctrine of the Prophets*, p. 277), contrasts the permanent with the precarious basis of righteousness, i.e. faith)(works. St Augustine contrasts the life of faith here with the life of sight hereafter for which it is the preparation.

peregrinatur...ex fide...speciem] A reminiscence of 2 Cor. v. 7 *dum sumus in corpore peregrinamur a Domino (per fidem enim ambulamus et non per speciem)*, i.e. we walk in an atmosphere of faith, not encompassed by the visible appearance of the glorified Christ, not seeing Him as He is, not looking upon His Face. *Species*, εἶδος practically = the direct vision of the reality itself)(the vision to the eye of faith through type, symbol, or sacrament. *Species* has the additional suggestion of glorious vision, which εἶδος lacks. Cp. *speciem candoremque coeli* (Cicero).

eorum...corda mundantur] *eorum* in the original connection refers to the Gentiles; here of course it is general.

si vides non est fides] Augustine seems to suggest that faith is only preparatory and transient, but St Paul's thought is that faith remains and is active even after the perfect vision has been vouchsafed. Cp. 1 Cor. xiii. 13 *nunc autem manent fides spes caritas.*

LXIX.
Page 16. § 1.

in eo quod audistis] *In eo* = abl. of instrument. See Hints on Grammar, p. 106.

dixerat enim superius Dominus, etc.] Note that the object of the first *dixerat*, viz. the quotation *et si abiero*, etc., is postponed until after the second, resumptive, *dixerat* (p. 18), and that all the sentences between the two are parenthetical.

ipsa Dei domus ipsi sunt] For *domus = templum = vos = communio sanctorum*, see note on *regnum Dei* lxviii. § 2.

Page 18. § 1.

quae in specie] See note on *speciem* lxviii. 3.

nescit ille mentiri...nesciebant] Augustine plays on two different meanings of *nescire* (1) to be ignorant, (2) to be unable.

Page 20. § 2.

ac per hoc] See Hints on Grammar, p. 106.

nisi enim credideritis non intelligetis] Vulg. *permanebitis*. See Table of Readings. Augustine's reconciliation of the two readings (*de Doctrina Christ.* ii. 17) is worth quoting in full, both as an illustration of his exegesis and of the esteem in which he was coming to hold Jerome's new translation, if, as is probable, he took *permanebitis* from it. (See Burkitt, *Old Latin and Itala*, p. 61.)

> *quoniam intellectus in specie sempiterna est, fides vero in rerum temporalium quibusdam cunabulis quasi lacte alit parvulos; nunc autem per fidem ambulamus, non per speciem, nisi autem per fidem ambulaverimus, ad speciem pervenire non poterimus quae non transit, sed permanet, per intellectum purgatum nobis cohaerentibus veritati: propterea ille ait, Nisi credideritis, non permanebitis; ille vero, Nisi credideritis non intelligetis.*

§ 3.

super me effundere animam meam] A recollection of Ps. xli. 5 (xlii. 4) *effudi in me animam meam.*

PAGE 22.

per hanc venisti manens ubi eras] The assumption of the human nature did not destroy the Godhead, the resumption of the full glory of the Godhead has not destroyed the humanity. Cp. Westcott's note on Hebr. x. 20.

alia Verbi alia est hominis persona] *Persona* first employed by Tertullian to express the eternal distinctions (ὑποστάσεις) in the divine nature. Hilary of Poitiers (A.D. 360) tried to use *substantia* in this sense, but in the time of these Homilies (A.D. 416) the terminology in the Western Church was fixed as *essentia* or *substantia* for substance (οὐσία), *persona* for person (ὑπόστασις). Cp. Gibson, *On the Thirty-nine Articles*, p. 111.

utrumque est Christus una persona] Cp. Athan. Creed, *v.* 32 and below lxxviii. 3 note.

aliquando enim Christus fuit mortuus] A recollection of 1 Pet. iii. 18.

PAGE 24. § 4.

accipite...exemplum] The human word and the divine Word which are here compared with each other are placed in contrast by Augustine in *Conf.* ix. 10: *Verbum (nostrum) et incipitur et finitur. Et quid simile verbo tuo domino nostro in se permanenti, etc.*

imago] Christ is the image of God (2 Cor. iv. 4; Col. i. 15).

Man is the image of God (1 Cor. xi. 7; Gen. i. 26).

non sunt corda...oneranda] For Augustine's consideration for his hearers, see Intr. § 2 (*b*).

LXX.

PAGE 26. § 1.

pristino sermone] viz. the last, § 2. *pristinus*, however, does not help us to fix the date of the delivery of *Tr.* lxix. as Augustine prefers *hesternus* (*sermo hesterni diei*) to denote 'yesterday's.'

quod itaque ait] Cp. *verum, quod tu dicis, mea uxor, non te mihi irasci decet* (Plautus *Amph.* 522).

sicut enim habet Pater vitam, etc.] The Father is the primal source of the divinity both of the Son and of the Holy Spirit (see Gibson, *On the Thirty-nine Articles*, pp. 115 ff.), but the Son is Himself a source of life for us (see Westcott on Jn. v. 26).

ad me ipsum turbata est anima mea] For the significance of the Hebrew עָלַי of which *ad me* and πρὸς ἐμαυτόν (LXX.) are literal renderings, see Kirkpatrick on Ps. xlii. 4 (*Cambridge Bible for Schools*).

PAGE 28. § 2.

si cognovistis...cognovistis...cognoscetis...vidistis] An O.L. reading (see Table) which does not correspond exactly to any extant Greek text, the nearest being that of ℵ (codex Sinaiticus), εἰ ἐγνώκατέ με καὶ τὸν πατέρα μου γνώσεσθε· ἀπ' ἄρτι γνώσεσθε αὐτὸν καὶ ἑωράκατε. The Vulg. (see Table of Readings) corresponds to the reading of the majority of Greek MSS. viz. εἰ ἐγνώκειτε...ἂν ᾔδειτε (*al.* ἐγνώκειτε ἄν)· ἀπ' ἄρτι γιγνώσκετε κ.τ.λ.

It is interesting to note that the Latin versions generally do not observe the distinction between οἶδα = *scio* and γινώσκω = *nosco, novi*. Thus Jn. vii. 28 κἀμὲ οἴδατε καὶ οἴδατε πόθεν εἰμί is rendered by the Vulg. *et me scitis et unde sim scitis*, by two O.L. texts *et me scitis et nostis unde sim*, and by five others *et me nostis et scitis unde sim*.

tanto tempore] See Hints on Grammar, p. 108.

ut quod ait] See note on *quod itaque ait* § 1.

PAGE 30.

alius enim ego sum alius ille] Cp. Athanasian Creed, *v.* 5.

Sabellianis......Patripassiani] Sabellius (A.D. 199—217) developed the teaching of Praxeas (A.D. 200) who maintained that the Son was personally one with the Father, and that it was therefore the Father who suffered on the cross in the character of the Son...*post tempus Pater natus et Pater passus*; hence the sobriquet by which these heretics were commonly known in the West, *Patripassiani*. See Gibson, *On the Thirty-nine Articles*, p. 106. Augustine's attack on Sabellianism is mainly academic, for it was practically a dead heresy by this time. Cp. *Ep.* cxviii. § 12, and *haeresis quippe ista nimis antiqua est, et paulatim eviscerata, Tr. in Ioan.* xl. 7.

§ 3.

quod si ad te multum est]= "if it is too much for thee" (cp. *multum est ad nos* lxxiv. 1). A possible rendering would be "if thou art greatly desirous"=*si multi facis*, but the context excludes it here.

PAGE 32.

quaeris videre] Cp. *contingere quaerunt* Lucr. iv. 1118; *mutare sedes quaerebant* Tac. *G.* 2.

LXXI.
§ 1.

audite auribus, accipite mentibus] Cp. lxvii. 1.

PAGE 34.

et verba opera sunt] A favourite thought of Augustine's in the Homilies. Cp. *Iesus cuius verba facta sunt* xxv. 2, and note the converse, *habent (miracula) linguam suam* xxiv. 2.

aedificat] See Hints on Grammar, p. 110.

Pater enim Deus non est de aliquo, etc.] Cp. Athanasian Creed, *vv.* 20, 21.

lumen de lumine] The phrase φῶς ἐκ φωτός, which survives in our so-called Nicene Creed, is most probably ante-Nicene in date and Origenistic in source. It was quoted by Eusebius at the Council of Nicaea in A.D. 325, almost certainly from an already existing creed. See Burn, *Introduction to the Creeds*, p. 78.

§ 2.

Ariani] Arianism, although defeated by the church and rejected by the Empire, survived in the West till the 6th century. Augustine had practical experience of it at Milan in the persecution of Ambrose by the Arian Empress Justina (see *Conf.* ix. 7), he died during the siege of Hippo by the Arian Vandals (see Intr., § 1), and he recognizes its danger and vitality in the same passage of the Homilies in which he speaks of Sabellianism as dead. *Arianorum autem adhuc videtur habere aliquas motiones quasi cadaveris putrescentis, aut certe ut multum quasi hominis animam agentis* (xl. 7). See above, note on *Sabellianis*, lxx. 2.

What the effect upon Christianity would have been if the false logic of the Arians had been allowed to prevail, is admirably stated by Gwatkin in *The Arian Controversy*, ch. 1.

Other passages of Scripture to which the Arians appealed in support of their contention are Prov. viii. 22; Mt. xxvi. 38, 39; xxvii. 46; Mk. xiii. 32; Lk. xviii. 19; xxiii. 43, 46; Jn. v. 19; xvii. 3; xx. 17.

Sabelliani] Tertullian declares that in the teaching of Praxeas, the real originator of this heresy (see on lxx. 2, note), *ipse deus, dominus omnipotens, Iesus Christus praedicatur (adv. Prax.* 1); that he held *filium carnem esse, patrem autem spiritum* (*ib.* 27), so that in a word *paracletum fugavit et patrem crucifixit* (*ib.* 1).

vos hinc, vos autem illinc, huc venite] Augustine, when preaching, generally deals gently with heretics (see however lxvii. 3), though he does not spare them in writing. He no doubt felt that the pulpit is not the place for acrid controversy.

This rhetorical mutual refutation of heresies is probably borrowed from Hilary (cp. *De Trin.* vii. 6), who in his turn may have taken the idea from Novatian (cp. *de Trin.* xxiii. *hoc in loco licebit mihi argumenta etiam ex aliorum haereticorum parte conquirere etc.*).

PAGE 36. § 2.

eum Arianus inaequalem asserat Patri] Their great error, viz. the inferiority of the Son as regards the essential nature of His Divinity, had its roots in a doctrine of subordination, which, although liable to misapprehension, is in itself, and as first propounded by Origen (and before him perhaps suggested by Tertullian, *pater tota substantia est, filius vero derivatio totius et portio*), theologically sound. See Bigg, *Christian Platonists*, pp. 181 ff.

quod ait, unum] See note on *quod itaque ait* lxx. 1.

bis unus] the Sabellian contention. See note on *Sabellianis* lxx. 2.

verum quia sic aequalis, etc.] This passage shews us the way in which Augustine does justice to the true doctrine of subordination. Derivation of being does not involve inequality of nature.

PAGE 38. § 3.

maiora horum] See Hints on Grammar, p. 107.

virtus] LXX. ἰσχύς. *virtus* is probably a survival of an O.L. rendering. There seems to have been a tendency to drop *virtus* as a translation of both ἰσχύς and δύναμις, for while it appears 68 times in R (Jerome's first revision of the Psalter), it occurs only 4 times in H (his last translation, from the Hebrew, see Intr. p. xiv), its place being generally taken by *fortitudo.* That St Augustine himself yielded to the tendency is shewn by his action in *Enarratio in Ps.* xvii., where he reads *virtus*, but explains it by *per quem fortis sum.* In quoting the verse here in close connection with Acts v. 15 he probably had in mind Lk. vi. 19, *quia virtus de illo exiebat et sanabat omnes.*

maius est enim, etc.] Augustine suggests, but without pressing it, a wrong account. It was not miracles of a more extraordinary, but of a different, viz. a spiritual kind, that our Lord promised to the believer, and this is admitted by Augustine a few lines further on—*haec sunt sine dubitatione maiora.*

eorundem verborum fructus erat fides] Cp. *Spem...quam audistis in verbo veritatis Evangelii quod...fructificat* (Col. i. 6) and the parable of the Sower.

gentes etiam crediderunt] *Gentes* is in contrast to *pauci* = whole nations, not merely the Gentiles.

LXXII.

PAGE 40. § 1.

pristino] See lxx. 1 note.

sine ipsis fecit et se ipsum] The thought, if not the actual expression, occurs more than once in the *de Trinitate* of Hilary of Poitiers (A.D. 356), e.g. *potente Verbo Deo ex se et carnem intra virginem assumere et carni animam tribuere* (x. 15); while to Augustine's *sine ipsis* corresponds Hilary's *non ex humana conceptione* (x. 18).

PAGE 42. § 2.

omnes ad suam familiam pertinentes] Cp. Collect for Good Friday (Sarum Missal from Gregorian Sacramentary), *Respice, Domine, quaesumus, super hanc familiam tuam.*

Familia denotes God's household the church. Cp. οἶκος in LXX. and N.T. (Num. xii. 7; Dt. xxiii. 1; Ps. lxviii. 9; Hos. viii. 1; ix. 15; Mt. x. 6; xv. 24; 1 Tim. iii. 15; 1 Pet. ii. 5; iv. 17; Hebr. iii. 2, 5, 6; viii. 8, 10; x. 21). The servile section of the household, which probably gave rise to the word (root FAM-, whence comes the Oscan *famel* and the Latin *famul, famulus* = slave), and to which it is often applied (cum insimularetur *familia*, partim etiam liberi, societatis eius, Cic.; *familiam* Catonianam vendere, Cic.), is not here in view, the thought being rather that of a whole great household, bond and free, united under one lord, *paterfamilias* (familia et pecunia Cic.; quorum princeps et caput paterfamilias vocatur, Nepos).

It is remarkable that although it occurs not less than 185 times in the Vulg. in a great variety of meanings, it is only used 4 times to render οἶκος absolutely, without qualifying words, such as πατρικός, πατρίων, κ.τ.λ., and that in spite of its obvious appropriateness St Jerome in no instance applies it, as St Aug. does here, to οἶκος Θεοῦ, but generally prefers *domus*, which is itself frequently used in classical writers in the sense of the household. (Cp. *domus* te nostra salutat, Cic.)

PAGE 44.

licet moriatur] Vg. *etiamsi mortuus fuerit* (see Table) which Aug. follows when he is preaching on the text in *Tr.* lxix. 15.

non toleratur nisi intelligatur] A notable rhetorical effect: "Intolerable! yes, until you understand."

iustificat...iustitiam] *Iustificare* = δικαιοῦν means throughout the Bible to pronounce or reckon righteous, not to make righteous. Augustine himself admits in one place that it *may* mean to reckon righteous...*sicut dictum est de quodam: Ille autem volens se iustificare; id est ut iustus haberetur et deputaretur* (*de Spiritu et Litera*, 45), but the exigencies of his controversy with the Pelagians, who said that a man could make himself righteous without God's grace, bound him to the other interpretation. The Pelagians denied the absolute necessity of grace in order to live a holy life; Augustine asserted it strongly, and appealed to St Paul. But in his exposition of Rom. v. etc., he practically abandoned the Apostle's theory of Justification for his own theory of Grace. His argument was that man is made righteous (*iustificatur*) by the grace of faith infused into him by God, which enables him to do works acceptable to God (*de Spiritu et Litera*, 18, 56). This thesis laid the foundation of one of the essential differences between the mediaeval doctrine (crystallized at the Council of Trent in 1547) and that of the Reformers. The Tridentine divines, following Augustine's teaching as developed by Thomas Aquinas, declared that justification meant infusion of grace as well as forgiveness of sins and so included sanctification; the Reformers, reverting to St Paul, held that justification meant forgiveness of sins alone, and that it was separable in thought, though not of course in fact, from sanctification. See Sanday and Headlam, *On Romans*, pp. 28 ff., 147 ff.

It is true that we have two words for the double meaning of *iustitia* = δικαιοσύνη, viz. "justice" and "righteousness," but to translate *iustificare* in this and the next section by "to render righteous," while it would make Augustine's meaning clear, would also obscure his somewhat arbitrary treatment of St Paul's theory.

in hoc opere faciamus, etc.] *Facimus* is a tempting emendation, but there is apparently no authority for the change.

PAGE 46. § 3.

sacramentum] This word has passed through several stages before reaching the sense in which it is used to-day. Starting with the meaning of something dedicated (root sac-=ἀγ-, see Sanday and Headlam, *On Romans*, p. 13), it came to denote self-dedication by way of oath or vow, then a promise or vow, and lastly a religious bond uniting the initiated. Μυστήριον, of which it is the recognised equivalent (as here), has a somewhat simpler history. It meant first a secret, then a religious secret, then a religious bond. Within these limits both words are employed by early Christian writers with studied vagueness. Thus we find τὸ μυστήριον = type or parable (Justin, *Tryph.* 40, 44, 78), the contents of the Gospel (Chrys. *in* 1 *Cor. hom.* vii.), a religious rite, e.g. Ordination (Greg. Naz. *Or.* i. *in sanct. Pascha*, 2), a church festival (Greg. Naz. *Or.* ii. 95), Baptism (Cyr. Hier. *Cat.* xviii. 32; Greg. Nyss. *Or cat. magn.* 33; Greg. Naz. *Or.* xl. *in sanct. bapt.* 28; Athan. *Or.* ii. c. *Ar.* 42), the Eucharist (Euseb. Caes. *de solemn. pasch.* 7, 9; Co. Laodic. canon 7); τὰ μυστήρια = religious rites (Origen *in Num. hom.* v. 1), Baptism and Eucharist (Cyr. Hier. *cat. myst.* i. 1; Chrys. *in Ioh. hom.* lxxxv. 3), Baptism (Greg. Naz. *Or. in diem lum.*), the Eucharist (Chrys. *ad illum. cat.* i. 2; ii. 2; Liturgies, *passim*), the holy Elements (Chrys. *de poenit.* ix.; Socr. *Hist. eccl.* ii. 38, cp. Ambros. *de excessu fratris sui*, 43); while *sacramentum* is applied to the military oath by Tertullian (*de Spect.* 24, *Scorp.* 4) and Cyprian (*de lapsis*, 13; *Ep.* lxxiv.), to any sacred rite by Tertullian (even to infanticide, with which the Christians were charged, *Apol.* 7), Cyprian and Augustine, to type and symbol or to any sacred thing which has a mysterious character by the same three writers, to church festivals by Augustine (*Ep.* lv.), to Baptism and the Eucharist either together or apart, in singular or plural, by many Latin writers, to the holy Elements by Ambrose and Augustine (*Serm.* ccxxvii., ccxxviii.; *de baptismo contra Donat.* ii. 104). The English translation must in every case be determined by the context.

Augustine's reason for quoting 1 Tim. iii. 16 here is the occurrence in it of *iustificatum est*. By *sacramentum pietatis* (τὸ μυστήριον τῆς εὐσεβείας) he understands Christ who, in his view, required grace, i.e. the Holy Spirit, for justification as much as we ourselves. See below lxxiv. 3, note on *Spiritus Domini super me*.

LXXIII.

PAGE 48. § 1.

unde homo] Note late extension of *unde* = whereby, cp. French *dont* = *de unde*.

quod culpabili concupiscentia petierunt] Numbers xi. 32. Cp. also Ps. lxxviii. 18 ff.

offensionem] *Offensio* primarily = (*a*) the physical act of stumbling. Hence it is applied (*b*) to the cause of stumbling and (*c*) to the psychological effect of stumbling, i.e. displeasure or anger. In Scripture, where so many metaphors describing conduct are taken from the idea of walking, 'stumbling' and 'falling' suggest further the idea of sin.

In the passage before us of course the only possible sense is (*c*), for God at least *irascitur, nescit autem peccare.*

Page 50.

quod dabat sapientia] *sapientia* = חָכְמָה, although personified in the Sapiential books, is nowhere in Scripture identified with God. It is His attribute and possession and practically = providence. The Apologists, however, constantly identify it with the Logos. So Hilary of Poitiers in the *de Trin.* (passim), though in *de Syn.*, interpreting Semiarianism, he speaks of it as a creature (*de Syn.* 17).

No theological argument can be based on Augustine's use of the word here, which is no doubt partly dictated by the assonance of *sapientia... concupiscentia.*

§ 2.

in sua promissione] See translation. *sua* might also mean "a promise made to them by His own lips."

Page 52. § 3.

Christus significat regem] Anointing with oil was the inaugural ceremony in ordering priests, prophets and kings, and *Christus*, with a qualifying word *domini, meus, tuus,* etc., is a common designation of a king in the O.T., e.g. 1 Sam. ii. 10; 2 Sam. i. 14; Ps. ii. 2; Is. xlv. 1.

Salvatorem] Cp. Mt. i. 21. The difficulty of Latin writers in finding an equivalent for σωτήρ is noteworthy (cp. *Sotera inscriptum vidi Syracusis; hoc quantum est? ita magnum ut Latine uno verbo exprimi non possit. Is est nimirum Soter qui salutem dedit.* Cicero *in Verrem,* ii. 63, 154) and justifies Augustine's fine saying, *salvare et salvator non fuerunt haec Latina; quando ad Latinos venit et haec Latine fecit* (*Serm.* ccxcix.). Various experiments in translation were made, *salutaris, salvificator* and even *salutificator* (Tert.), before *salvator* was finally fixed by Jerome.

LXXIV.

Page 56. § 1.

multum...ad nos] See lxx. 3, note on *si ad te multum est.*
Spiritum Paracletum] See below § 4 note.

consubstantialem et coaeternum] *Consubstantialis* = ὁμοούσιος is used by Tertullian (*adv. Hermogenem* 44). The word was therefore sanctioned as a theological term by the Western Church before Augustine, and its application to the Holy Spirit probably dates from the latter half of the 4th century, when the question of His coessential deity began to be seriously discussed. Cp. the decision of the 2nd Roman Synod under Damasus in A.D. 369, that the Holy Spirit must be regarded as of the same substance as the Father and the Son; and on the whole subject consult Gwatkin, *The Arian Controversy*, p. 124, and Swete, *Early History of the Doctrine of the Holy Spirit*, p. 50.

Coaeternus is predicated of the Spirit in the *Fides Romanorum* attributed to Phaebadius of Agen († A.D. 392).

Page 58.

eo modo...quo...intelligi voluit] i.e. professing full allegiance to Christ with all that it involves, for *fides* implies *amor*. Cp. below, *nemo sic dicit nisi qui diligit*, and lxvii. 1, note on *in Deum*.

iam itaque apostoli dicebant...] Augustine does not say when the Spirit was first bestowed; he only argues that He must have been present already in some degree for the Apostles to make profession of loving allegiance to Christ.

Page 60. § 2.

postea ab ipso missus...] viz. at Pentecost. In Jn. xv. 26 our Lord speaks of the Spirit as sent by Himself.

hoc est proximi et Dei] For *dilectio proximi* cp. Lev. xix. 18; for *dilectio Dei* cp. Mt. xxiii. 37 and parallels; Rom. xiii. 9.

sanctus Elisaeus sancto Eliae] *sanctus* is not used here in the technical modern sense of 'saint,' of which the nearest early equivalent was *dominus*, *domina*. It does not appear as a title = saint)(attribute = holy, before the middle of the 5th century. It is perhaps to be regretted that the Church of England, when forming her Kalendar, did not include in it saints of the Old as well as of the New Covenant.

§ 3.

de ipso Dei Filio loquebatur] Both Augustine and the translators of the A.V. are probably wrong in making the Son the sole recipient of the unmeasured gift of the Spirit. The Baptist's statement in Jn. iii. 34 is a general one and there is no warrant or reason for restricting it to the Son of God alone.

Spiritus Domini super me, etc.] Our Lord in quoting this verse of *Isaiah* evidently connected it with His baptism (Lk. iv. 1, 14, 18). Augustine thinks rather of the Incarnation (as is clear from his reference to 1 Tim. ii. 5), and uses the passage to defend an important theological position. The Father alone is *fons gratiae* in the absolute sense (see above lxx. 1, note on *sicut enim habet Pater vitam*); Christ is only *fons gratiae* relatively to man. Thus it was no less the work of grace that His humanity was taken up into union with His divinity, enabling Him to live a perfect human life, than it is a gift of grace which enables us to live lives of obedience and holiness. See above lxxii. 3, note on *sacramentum.*

assumptus est homo] Cp. Athanasian Creed, *v.* 33. *Homo = natura humana,* cp. below lxxviii. 3 and Hilary *Tr. in Ps.* liii., etc.

gratia Dei erat in illo] Augustine takes *gratia,* not as the goodwill which the Father had towards the Son because of His willing obedience, but as the enabling power of grace. Cp. last note but one.

donec unicuique...propria mensura compleatur] Augustine evidently has in mind *donec occurramus omnes...in virum perfectum, in mensuram aetatis plenitudinis Christi* (Eph. iv. 13) according to what is probably the right interpretation, viz. the perfecting of the individual life, although it is sometimes applied to the perfecting of the church. See Abbott, *On Ephesians, ad loc.*

§ 4.

ostendit et se ipsum esse Paracletum] Although Augustine was no Greek scholar (cp. *ego quidem Graecae linguae perparum assecutus sum et prope nihil...contra litt. Petil.* ii. 37, 1, and for his early hatred of the language see *Conf.* i. 14), he knew enough to be able to deal with isolated words.

Rufinus, the translator of Origen, distinguishes between παράκλητος in its application to Christ and to the Spirit, giving it in the former case the sense of *deprecator* = advocate, 'counsel for the defence' (as here), and in the latter, that of *consolator* = comforter *(de Princip.* ii. 7).

prudentia carnis] φρόνημα σαρκός, Vulg. *sapientia,* but in the previous verse of Rom. viii. *prudentia.* It is interesting to recall Cicero's definition of *prudentia* and *sapientia. Prudentia quam Graeci φρόνησιν vocant est rerum expetendarum fugiendarumque scientia; sapientia autem ...rerum divinarum humanarumque scientia. De Off.* i. 43. Neither is a satisfactory representative of φρόνημα, which means what one has in mind, the general bent of thought and motive. The inadequacy of the

Latin and the difficulty of finding an English equivalent are testified by the language of the Bishops' Bible (A.D. 1568) "φρονοῦσι and φρόνημα... do not so much signify wisdom and prudence, as affection, carefulness, and minding of anything" (note on Rom. viii. 6) and that of Art. ix. *affectus carnis Graece φρόνημα σαρκός quod alii sapientiam, alii sensum, alii studium carnis interpretantur.*

LXXV.

PAGE 64. § 1.

orphani pupilli sunt] For Augustine's knowledge of Greek see note on *Paracletus* lxxiv. 4.

We are here confronted with terms and ideas taken from Roman law. *pupillus -a* was the technical word for a child who needed protection and defence of legal rights. To this end *tutores* were appointed (*appellantur tutores quasi tuitores atque defensores,* Justinian), who by their *auctoritas* supplied (*augebant*) the deficiency of their wards. It may be remarked that 'pupils'=orphans is used by Jeremy Taylor in the *Holy Living*, ch. 3, § 2, 'pupils and widows.'

PAGE 66. § 1.

quamvis nos...Filius, etc.] The idea of adoption (*adoptio, υἱοθεσία*), although familiar to us from its presence in the N.T., is really rather difficult for English readers to apprehend in its fulness, because it has no place in our law and hardly one in our custom. It has however a most important feature in all early systems (see Maine, *Ancient Law*, pp. 134 ff.), and afforded in Apostolic times an illustration of one aspect of the relation between God and man. The Latin fathers are sometimes blamed for their theological application of forensic terms, but in this case at least they only followed the example of St Paul. See Rom. viii. 15, 23; ix. 4; Gal. iv. 5; Eph. i. 5.

Filius Dei suo patri] To predicate adoption directly of the Son is forbidden alike by theology (cp. Ephes. i. 5 προορίσας ἡμᾶς εἰς υἱοθεσίαν διὰ Ἰησοῦ Χριστοῦ εἰς αὐτόν, sc. τὸν θεὸν καὶ πατέρα κ.τ.λ.), and by the analogy of Roman law. The tutor might not adopt to himself, but he would be discharging a natural and proper function in finding a suitable guardian for his wards.

ipse circa nos paternum affectum...demonstrat] On Christ's paternal relation towards His disciples see Jn. x. 14; xiii. 23 (τεκνία); xvii. 23, with Westcott's notes.

sponsi filios nos appellat] The Latin translations of Mt. ix. 15, unless they were following the Western reading (D) τοῦ νυμφίου, misrepresent the Greek text. οἱ υἱοὶ τοῦ νυμφῶνος = wedding guests, must not be confounded with ὁ φίλος τοῦ νυμφίου = groomsman. See art. 'Bridegroom' in Hastings's *Dict. of Bible*.

In any case Augustine's interpretation is based on a misconception of the phrase, for the Hebraism בני חופה, represented by οἱ υἱοὶ τοῦ νυμφῶνος, does not denote a filial relation but merely close connection. Cp. sons of Belial = base fellows; son of affliction = a man greatly afflicted; son of fatness = very fruitful.

§ 2.

carnem suam...noluit demonstrare non suis] There was a general agreement in the early church that the Risen Christ was seen by His friends alone, but the reasons alleged for the restriction are various, and illustrate in an instructive way the difference in temper between Eastern and Western theologians. Thus, while Origen and Chrysostom held that Christ withheld Himself from the eyes of His foes from a desire not to increase their guilt and to save them from being struck blind, Tertullian declared that it was in order to prevent their repentance and forgiveness.

Westcott points out that a vision of the glorified Saviour was granted to one of His enemies, viz. Saul. Cp. *Revelation of the Risen Lord*, pp. 11, 194.

§ 3.

et quia ipsius...vivetis] Augustine falls short of the whole truth when he tries to restrict the life, whether of Christ or of believers, to the life after death. Christ *is* the Life, and to them that believe a source and assurance of endless life, and that not only of the body, as Augustine takes it here, but of the whole being.

PAGE 68.

quia nos viximus] This is the MS. reading. Editors have endeavoured to bring out the full force of Aug.'s thought, viz. that exaltation of self was the cause of death's entry into the world, by substituting *nobis* for *nos*.

§ 4.

in quo die, etc.] 'That' day began with Pentecost and reaches its consummation at the second Advent. Cp. Jn. xvi. 23, 26, Westcott's notes.

speciem] See lxviii. 3, note.

PAGE 70. § 5.

nunc enim ad hoc dilexit] "to the end" (see translation) is perhaps ambiguous as recalling Jn. xiii. 1, A.V. and R.V. text. Render 'in order that.' The phrase is a good example of *ut* needing to be fortified to make it final.

LXXVI.

PAGE 72. § 1.

cuius epistola inter Scripturas canonicas legitur] The earliest application of the words κανών, κανονίζειν, κανονικός to the body of Holy Scripture occurs in the writings of Athanasius (Festal Epistle, A.D. 367), although the conception of a rule or standard by which books claiming inspiration were measured is long anterior (see art. 'Canon' in Hastings's *Dict. of the Bible*). What Augustine's Canonical Scriptures precisely were is difficult to ascertain because of his varying language and uncertain usage (see Gibson, *On the Thirty-nine Articles*, p. 256), but it is probable that he included among them the O.T. Apocrypha, whereas Jerome definitely excluded them. It is certain that the Council of Carthage in A.D. 397, at which he was probably present, adopted the Canon of the LXX., including the Apocrypha, and it is to this Council, and therefore largely to Augustine's influence, that the position of the Apocrypha in the Western Church is principally due.

There was special reason for emphasizing the claims to canonicity for the Epistle of Jude, as it seems to have fallen out of use in the African Church, although it had early found acceptance there. See art. 'Jude' in Hastings's *Dict. of the Bible*.

§ 2.

quia diligunt eliguntur] Election here has its ground in love evinced by man towards God, but there is nothing inconsistent in this passage with Augustine's constant teaching on the subject, for the love itself is grounded on a prior gift from the Father *qui donat et ipsam dilectionem*. See Intr. § 1.

omnia sacramenta] = μυστήρια. See note on *sacramentum*, lxxii. 3.

dilectio sanctos discernit a mundo] Saints dwell together in the House of God; sinners remain outside.

PAGE 74.

quae nec talis est, etc.] Augustine is probably not thinking of the Last Judgement, but of the judgement caused by the coming of the Light into the world (Jn. iii. 19). Cp. *Tr.* xliv. 17.

§ 3.

§ 3 is apparently not a strict development of the argument of § 2, but an afterthought suggested by *ad modicum tempus*.

nemo illorum vidit eum] See note on *carnem suam...noluit demonstrare non suis*, lxxv. 2.

credimus...ad iudicium...esse venturum] Cp. *Iudex crederis esse venturus* in the Te Deum (*v.* 19) which, without accepting the tradition assigning its composition to Augustine and Ambrose, we may very well believe them to have known. See Burn, *Intr. to the Creeds*, ch. xi.

in eodem corpore] Cp. Gibson on Article iv., and Westcott, *Gospel of the Resurrection*; Milligan, *Lectures on the Resurrection*.

PAGE 76. § 4.

subveniendo...obediendo, etc.] Gerunds of manner, not of purpose.

in forma hominis] "Because of the three Persons which are God, He only is also the Son of man ; and therefore for His affinity with their nature, for His sense of their infirmities, on His appearance to their eyes, most fit to represent the greatest mildness and sweetness of equity, in the severity of that just and irrespective judgement." Pearson, *On the Creed*, p. 513 ff.

§ 5.

et fortasse propter aliquam distinctionem] *fortasse* indicates a certain hesitation in pressing what is the only piece of fanciful interpretation in these thirteen Homilies. See Intr. p. ix.

With regard to *sermo* and *verbum* (sc. *Dei*), notice that while Tertullian varies, like Augustine, in his usage, Cyprian always has *sermo*.

LXXVII.

PAGE 78. § 1.

manebit] *manere* = dwell, cp. English mansions.

in sanctis tamquam in templo suo] For the Church = House of God, see lxviii. 1 note.

illa spiritalis est atque intrinsecus mentibus redditur] The right of *mens* to represent πνεῦμα, the highest power of man's nature, may be gathered from Cicero's statement, *mens cui regnum totius animi a natura tributum est*, taken in connection with the definitions of a late grammarian, Nonius, *animus est quo sapimus, anima qua vivimus*.

PAGE 80. § 2.

commemorabit vos] Vg. *suggeret vobis* (see Table) which is the reading adopted by Aug. in *Tr.* civ. 1. Cp. above *Tr.* lxxii. 2, note on *licet moriatur*.

Trinitas ipsa dicat et doceat] The whole of this section with its strong assertion of inseparable unity is important. We are sometimes apt to forget that the object of Christian adoration is a Triune God, and to destroy the right balance and proportion of our worship by isolating the Persons.

PAGE 82.

saluberrimos monitus ad gratiam pertinere, etc.] For Augustine's doctrine of preventing grace—to him we owe the term *gratia praeveniens* —see Intr. § 1, and Bright, *Anti-Pelagian Treatises*, Introd. p. 19.

Note strange use of *commemorare* with double accusative, cp. *Confess.* i. 7.

§ 3.

pacem super pacem] See Table, p. xxiii.

ne de occultis nostris invicem iudicemus] Cp. below, § 4, *itemque inter nos ipsos est nobis pax.*

A censorious and suspicious temper is inconsistent even with the measure of peace available for us, with our half knowledge of each other, on earth; *a fortiori* with the perfect peace and unveiled vision which will be ours hereafter, when the cause of fault-finding is removed.

§ 4.

non addidit meam] *meam* is however added in a number of MSS., both of O.L. and Vulg. See *Oxford Edition, ad loc.*

PAGE 84.

itemque inter nos ipsos, etc.] See above, § 3, note on *ne de occultis,* etc.

PAGE 86. § 5.

cor unum sursum habeamus]

sursum corda...habemus ad dominum

ἄνω τὸν νοῦν...ἔχομεν πρὸς τὸν Κύριον

introduce the Preface in the Communion Service in every known liturgy.

LXXVIII.

§ 1.

Christus homo et Deus] Cp. Athanasian Creed, *v.* 28.

ibat...manebat] For the sense in which Christ may be said to be everywhere present, even as man, cp. Hooker, *Eccl. Polity*, Bk. v. ch. 55, Paget, *Introduction*, pp. 147 ff., and Aug. *Ep.* clxxxvii.

132 NOTES.

PAGE 88.

Deus...qui nullo continetur loco] Cp. Οὐ γὰρ ἐν γνόφῳ ἢ τόπῳ ὁ Θεός, ἀλλὰ ὑπεράνω καὶ τόπου καὶ χρόνου καὶ τῆς τῶν γεγονότων ἰδιότητος. Clem. Alex. *Strom.* ii. 2.

mente] See above, lxxvii. 1.

non forma Dei recessit] For a strong statement of the doctrine cp. Hilary, *Tr. in Ps.* liii.

haec est assumpta] Cp. lxxiv. 3, note.

§ 2.

neque enim homo Christus non dicitur Filius Dei, etc.] The doctrine of the *communicatio idiomatum*, for which see Hooker, *Eccl. Polity*, Bk. v. ch. 53.

PAGE 90.

maior est Pater, secundum id quod Verbum caro factum est] It is in the Incarnation that Augustine commonly finds the superior greatness of the Father, and this view became general, almost universal, in the West (see Westcott, *On St John, ad loc.*), but Augustine admits the truth of the doctrine of Subordination (see notes on *Ariani* etc., lxxi. 2), *illa* (Jn. xiv. 28, etc.) *posita sunt, partim propter administrationem suscepti hominis...partim propter hoc quia Filius Patri debet quod est, hoc etiam debens utique Patri quod eidem Patri aequalis aut par est ; Pater autem nulli debet, quidquid est. De Fide et Symbolo,* 18.

Eunomiani] The extremest sect of Arians, taking their name from their leader Eunomius, Bishop of Cyzicus (flor. A.D. 360). Also known as Anomoeans (ὁ Υἱὸς παντελῶς ἀνόμοιός ἐστι τῷ Πατρί), and Exoukontians (ἐξ οὐκ ὄντων ἐκτίσθη ὁ λόγος). See Gwatkin, *Arian Controversy*, p. 75.

PAGE 92. § 3.

non duo sed unus est Christus] The language of the Athan. Creed, v. 32. See above, lxix. 3, note.

quaternitas] Probably a direct reference to the Nestorian heresy, which introduced a fourth Person, the man Christ Jesus united to the Personal Word, into the Godhead, and so practically substituted a Quaternity for the Trinity. For the effect it would have had, if sanctioned, upon the doctrine of the Atonement, see Hooker, *Eccl. Polity*, Bk. v. ch. 53, § 3, and Gibson, *On the Thirty-nine Articles*, p. 136.

It was condemned by the Council of Ephesus in A.D. 431, but the Council of Chalcedon in A.D. 451, primarily concerned as it was with Eutychianism, dealt a final blow to the earlier heresy, against which the later was a kind of reaction. Thus the Chalcedonian Definition of Faith states as catholic doctrine, ῝Εν πρόσωπον τοῦ Κυρίου ἐν δύο φύσεσιν, ἀσυγχύτως, ἀτρέπτως (against Eutyches), ἀδιαιρέτως, ἀχωρίστως (against Nestorius). The followers of Peter the Fuller (flor. A.D. 490) were known as τετραδίται, quaternitatem tenentes.

sicut enim unus est homo…sic unus est Christus Deus et homo]
This illustration of the union of the two natures in the one Person of Christ by analogy of the union of soul and flesh in man, is common in the fathers from A.D. 350 to 450, and is employed, among others besides Augustine, by Gregory of Nazianzus, Vincentius of Lerins, and Cyril of Alexandria. But it became discredited by the sense put upon it by the Eutychians (Monophysites, see Robertson, ii. 270 ff.), who argued that as soul and body form but one nature in man, so they can form but one nature in Christ; and from the Council of Chalcedon (A.D. 451) onwards it ceased to be used by orthodox writers except as a phrase to be condemned or carefully guarded.

Its presence in the Athanasian Creed (v. 35) is an argument in favour of a pre-Eutychian date for that Symbol, as the fathers of the Council of Chalcedon, which condemned Eutyches, would hardly have allowed the insertion into a Catholic Creed of what experience taught them was a dangerous clause. See Waterland, *History of Ath. Cr.*, p. 147; Burn, *Intr. to the Creeds*, p. 141.

eo quod sic assumpta est] Cp. above, § 1, and lxxiv. 3, note.

LXXIX.
PAGE 94. § 1.

calumniosis et dementibus] *calumnia* is a regular term in Roman law for malicious accusation. Cp. Lk. xix. 8, where for the *defraudavi* of Vg.=ἐσυκοφάντησα, Codex Bezae reads *calumniavi*, and Tertullian has *per calumniam eripui*; but the word is probably not used in any technical sense here.

vident et credunt] Vg. *viderunt et crediderunt* (see Table), the reading which Aug. adopts in *Tr.* cxxi. 5. Cp. above *Tr.* lxxii. 2; lxxvii. 2, notes.

epistola quae scribitur ad Hebraeos] Augustine nowhere directly asserts the Pauline authorship of Hebrews, but he often uses 'the Apostle' to denote its writer, and in one connection at least in a way that can only refer to St Paul. Cp. *Expos. Epist. ad Rom.* 18, 19.

For the history of its admission into the canon of the Western Church, see Salmon, *Introduction to the N.T.*, pp. 417 ff.

9—3

fides sperantium substantia] Cp. *Tr.* xlv. 2. It is difficult to see how this reading (that of *r* = codex Freisingensis) arose, as there is apparently no MS. authority for ἐλπιζόντων, and the Middle of ἐλπίζω is very rare. *d* = codex Claromontanus and *e* = codex Petropolitanus have *isperantium substantia rerum, accusator non videntium*.

substantia] ὑπόστασις = resolute confidence. Cp. 2 Cor. ix. 4; xi. 17; Hebr. iii. 14, on which see Westcott's note.

PAGE 96.

viventem et ad Patrem ascendentem] Augustine refers to the act of Ascension (Lk. xxiv. 51; Acts i. 9), though, as Westcott points out, the tense of ἀναβαίνω, *ascendo* in Jn. xx. 17 implies that the ascent to the Father began with the renewed life of the risen Lord, and thus the words would have a meaning if applied to the whole of the Forty Days.

cum resurrexisset refecta] See Westcott, *Revelation of the Risen Lord*, p. 115, and Latham, *Pastor Pastorum*, ch. xiii.

PAGE 98. § 2.

tenebrarum harum] In Eph. vi. 12; Col. i. 13, *tenebrae* = σκότος describes a state of darkness; in Eph. v. 8, persons in that state. Augustine takes it in the latter sense in both instances.

de peccati propagine] *propago* = the race, breed or stock to which a creature belongs (cp. Munro on Lucretius iii. 741).

For the doctrine, cp. Jn. i. 13, and οὐκ ἔστιν ὁ Χριστὸς ἄνθρωπος ἐξ ἀνθρώπων κατὰ τὸ κοινὸν τῶν ἀνθρώπων γεννηθείς (Justin M., *Dial. cum Tryph.* 54).

PAGE 100.

quae non rapui, tunc exsolvebam] An expression (perhaps proverbial) for the extreme of injured innocence. See Kirkpatrick *ad loc.*

Augustine plays on the etymological connection of *rapere* with *rapina* in Phil. ii. 7. See on *Tr.* lxvii. 1.

ut incommunicabile nomen...divinitatis invaderet] Cp. *eritis sicut Dei*, Gen. iii. 5. Adam thought to gain equality with God; he only won that which put God out of his reach.

INDEX TO NOTES.

The references are to pages of the introductory and explanatory notes and the hints on grammar. Latin words which occur in the commentary are recorded, but the Vocabulary on pp. 109, 110 is intended to serve as a general *Index Latinitatis*, while the Table of Readings on pp. xix—xxxix stands for an Index of Texts.

Exoukontians 132

For EU product safety concerns, contact us at Calle de José Abascal, 56–1°,
28003 Madrid, Spain or eugpsr@cambridge.org.